# Rebellion Town

# BY THE AUTHOR

Air Raid—Pearl Harbor!
*The Story of December 7, 1941*
Rebellion Town
*Williamsburg, 1776*

973.3
T

# REBELLION TOWN,
# Williamsburg, 1776

## BY THEODORE TAYLOR
*Drawings by Richard Cuffari*

Thomas Y. Crowell Company         New York

*The map on pages 34 and 35 is by Miklos Pinther*

Manufactured in the United States of America

**Library of Congress Cataloging in Publication Data**

Taylor, Theodore, date
  Rebellion town.

  Bibliography: p.
  SUMMARY: Traces the events which led to the Declaration of Independence, with emphasis on the events in Williamsburg, Virginia.
  1. United States—History—Revolution—Causes—Juvenile literature.   2. Virginia—Politics and government—Colonial period, c. 1600–1775—Juv. lit.   [1. United States—History—Revolution—Causes.     2. Virginia—Politics and government—Colonial period]   I. Cuffari, Richard, illus.   II. Title.

E210.T39     973.3′11     73-10187
ISBN 0-690-00019-7

1 2 3 4 5 6 7 8 9 10

*To Phyllis and George Seaton*

With gratitude for so many things, most of
all, warmth of friendship

# Acknowledgments

*Motion-picture writer and director George Seaton, who made a fine film on Williamsburg, suggested this book. Colonial Williamsburg, Inc., made it possible. I'm especially grateful to Dr. Jane Carson of the research staff at Williamsburg for her assistance and advice.*

# Contents

# Rebellion Town

# 1 Roots of Rebellion

Rebellion against a government has to begin somewhere, but on this peaceful morning, with the fra-
grance of spring filling the air, there is no indication it will take root here in the small town of
Williamsburg, the capital of Virginia Colony.
Even the wildest imagination could not have fore-
cast that a comparatively unknown country lawyer

named Patrick Henry would strike the first verbal match to inflame thirteen British colonies; that the fire he starts will smolder and then burn brightly eleven years hence in Philadelphia, finally exploding in the Declaration of Independence.

In this third week of May, 1765, it would be ridiculous even to mention the idea of separation from England. After all, the colonies in America have had a relatively good relationship with the mother country for more than a hundred years, enjoying great freedoms. Although they mostly govern themselves, the colonists nevertheless feel a deep loyalty to the homeland, and there are family and business ties linking the people an ocean apart.

But, undeniably, there has been angry talk lately. England's new revenue plan, the dreaded Stamp Act, is to take effect in the fall. For the first time the colonists will be directly taxed by the British Parliament. The fees will reach into the purses of every man and woman.

For years the colonists have been assessed internally by their own legislative assemblies to pay for the cost of government. The assemblies have jealously guarded this right to levy taxes and none of the revenue has been returned to England. The Stamp Act not only challenges that this right, which is self-claimed, belongs solely to the assemblies, but sets a precedent for future taxation by the Crown.

Virginia Colony, in particular, has always been sensitive about tax matters—and sometimes unreasonable. In 1717, for example, Parliament had moved to establish a biweekly postal system between Williamsburg and Philadelphia, with the local postage rates to be paid by Virginians. It was a progressive, worthy move and some northern colonies had already accepted the system. But Virginia stubbornly refused the mail route, viewing the postage rates as taxes. The decision was not too surprising. Ninety-eight years earlier the first General Assembly of Virginia had displayed hardheaded independence, claiming for itself the sole right to tax the people.

The 1718 General Assembly passed a law defeating the postal system, but Governor Alexander Spotswood refused to sign the measure and the mail route was established. Williamsburg fumed then as it was fuming now.

During the whole of the past summer, when the General Assembly had been in adjournment, the Stamp Act issue had festered in Virginia and in the other colonies, too. There was outrage in Massachusetts and Rhode Island; South Carolina and North Carolina were indignant. Everywhere, the measure was the subject of talks and protests.

England said that the tax was designed to help pay for the costly, grueling French and Indian Wars, which had ended in 1759, with peace formally declared in 1763. That war, pitting England against France and France's American Indian allies, had been fought in defense of the colonies, initially to prevent France from linking her Canadian territory with her colony of Louisiana, far to the south. Had France been successful, her territory would have extended along the entire western border of the British colonies.

Additionally, some officials in England had long thought that America should pay direct taxes to the mother country. Why shouldn't her citizens be charged for their own administration and defense? It was a reasonable argument. Ten thousand British troops, some of them veterans of the French and Indian Wars, remained in America as a defensive force.

The issue had first arisen the previous year with Parliament's passage of the Sugar Act, which extracted customs duties, payable to the Crown, on a number of imported products, including sugar. The small fees resulted in higher prices for sugar and other products, and this was, of course, a financial blow to colonial merchants who were still struggling out of the postwar business depression. Massachusetts, always quick to rise if colonial rights were challenged, had led the protests against this revenue bill.

Although higher prices resulted from the Sugar Act, the tax itself, paid by the merchant, was invisible to the average citizen. But the fees to be paid under the Stamp Act would be very visible and direct, an "external" tax for the first time. In its fifty-four provisions, the law would extract a "stamp fee" on every conceivable legal document as well as on newspapers, calendars, advertisements, even packs of playing cards. Each item would be affixed with a "stamp," paid for by the consumer at time of sale.

The proposed duty on some items was particularly galling. Since many prominent Virginia blue-bloods loved to gamble, the contemplated tax on dice, for example, caused some temperatures to rise—imagine the snit of the eminent Colonel William Byrd, III, "rattling the bones" at Mrs. Vobe's tavern, also known as The King's Arms, in Williamsburg, had he paid a duty to the Crown for his pleasure.

And if the Stamp Act was not repealed, what

would be taxed next? Land? Even the privilege of voting could be taxed. That, too, had been mentioned in London. From the colonial viewpoint, the tariff gave England a frightening foot in the door.

But beyond the cost to the colonists of present and future proposals for raising revenue was an issue of far more consequence: Did England have a constitutional right to tax her American colonies without their consent? Without the specific approval of each general assembly in the colonies, the elected local governing body?

The past November, Richard Henry Lee, a member of the House of Burgesses, the lower house of Virginia's General Assembly, had introduced a resolution calling for a committee to draft a "Petition to the King, a Memorial to the House of Lords, and a Remonstrance to the House of Commons." The House of Lords and the House of Commons were the upper and lower houses of Parliament in London. Each document would protest the Stamp Act.

Men whose names were very familiar in Virginia politics formed the committee: Peyton Randolph, who was the chairman; Edmund Pendleton, George Wythe, Richard Bland, Richard Henry Lee, and John Fleming. To the brilliant lawyer

George Wythe fell the task of drafting the most important paper, "the Remonstrance," or complaint, to the British House of Commons.

The sole purpose of the three documents was to persuade Parliament to soften, if not entirely abandon, the Stamp Act proposals. In drawing up such resolutions, the colonists were acting according to customary constitutional procedure. The governing of the colonies had always been more or less a matter of cooperation, although the King and Parliament had the last say.

Wythe's original wording was apparently too tough for some of his more timid, conservative colleagues to swallow, Pendleton in particular. So the complaint was watered down. In fact, all three documents, in final form, were polite, almost apologetic, and did not truly represent the feeling in Williamsburg or in the other colonies.

Yet one statement in the complaint addressed to the House of Commons went straight to the point: ". . . it is essential to British liberty that laws imposing Taxes on the people ought not to be made without Consent of the Representatives chosen by themselves . . ."

Although many citizens continued to express their wrath during the winter, and were still doing so even now, in the spring, it was evident that the colonies would probably bow to Parliament and King George, however grudgingly. The citizens did not know, of course, that Patrick Henry, a lean fiddle-playing man of coarse appearance, the newly elected burgess from Hanover County, was awaiting an opportunity to unleash a startling attack on the Stamp Act and the Crown itself.

# 2 The House of Burgesses

On May 21st the bronze bell in the steeple of stately Bruton Parish Church rings out. Soon, the members of the House of Burgesses move along Duke of Gloucester Street, the main street of Williamsburg, toward the Capitol. Arriving, they file into the lobby and on into the hall.

The oldest legislative body in America, the

House of Burgesses dates back to the summer of 1619 when Sir George Yeardley, "Knight, Governor and Captain General of Virginia Colony," sent summonses throughout the countryside asking each borough or district to choose two representatives to serve in the lower house of the new government. His own Council, its members selected by the Crown, would serve as the upper house. On or about July 30th, the two bodies, now known as the General Assembly, met for the first time in Jamestown. The groups have been meeting with some regularity ever since.

Interestingly enough, the system of government has not changed very much throughout the years. Measures passed by the House of Burgesses go to the upper house, or the King's Council, whose members are usually aristocrats appointed for life, for approval or disapproval. If the Council and then the governor endorse the bills, they go to Parliament for final approval.

The hall in which the delegates are gathering today is not particularly large. It is dominated at the upper end by a dais and a high-backed wooden chair, on which the speaker of the house sits. On either side of the room are two long wooden benches for the burgesses. There is also a clerk's

desk, with inkwells and a quill pen. Few frills grace this hall.

Robed and wigged, the speaker of the house, the presiding officer and parliamentarian, is the rich, aging conservative John Robinson. A planter with large landholdings, he has held this powerful post since 1735 and is also treasurer of the colony. Deeply entrenched, he, more than anyone else, represents Virginia's aristocracy.

Sometimes by dress and bearing alone, one can tell the political interests of the burgesses. The planters, often resplendent in silk and satin, tend to be conservative. They have traditionally held the power. The back-country men, like Patrick Henry, are usually dressed simply and are apt to be more liberal and progressive. They would like to exert more power in this hall but so far have lacked a leader.

So, to look at the men as they enter and move about, applying friendly smiles or cool stares, is to see both the shine of plantation wealth and the simplicity of the wilderness and mountains. This mixture can also be glimpsed along Duke of Gloucester Street at any hour of the day.

Richard Bland has been a burgess for fifteen years. His family dates back to the earliest settlers. It is no surprise that he is a conservative. Another staunch conservative is the lawyer Edmund Pendleton, from Caroline County, a tall man in his midforties. Unlike Bland, he rose from obscurity.

There have been prominent Randolphs in Virginia for a century and portly Peyton Randolph is very much present this day. Next to Robinson, he is probably the most influential politician in the colony. It is no secret that he will likely succeed Robinson as speaker.

Not so conservative are such well-to-do men as Richard Henry Lee, George Wythe, John Fleming, and George Washington. Lee, in particular, has always seemed ready for a good fight with the Crown, although he is loyal to British rule, as are all of the burgesses assembling.

During the past months Colonel Washington may well have paused now and then to think of a place called Fort Necessity in the Ohio Valley. There, on the Great Meadows, he had surrendered the Virginia militia to the French in 1754. A surveyor, he had been sent as second-in-command of three hundred expeditionary troops, authorized by this same Assembly, to drive the French out of the valley. The action started the French and Indian Wars, which, in turn, brought on the Stamp Act.

He had ridden back from the Ohio seven years before deciding that soldiering wasn't for him; he had married the widow Martha Custis, and in February, 1759, he had become a burgess. He is a striking man, hard-muscled and arrow straight. His dark brown hair is worn in a queue.

Patrick Henry, the freshman burgess, was sworn in about May 20th, joining the session almost three weeks after it had convened. His face is like a dark wedge, long and thin, more sallow than ruddy. His forehead is high and straight. The nose is long. His hair has darkened somewhat from its youthful reddish brown. Although most burgesses have heard about him, few have ever seen him before now.

Among those who have met him are Peyton Randolph and George Wythe. Five years ago, Henry had ridden into Williamsburg, hoping to obtain a license to practice law. Although his formal schooling had stopped at the age of ten, he had been tutored by his well-educated Scots father, and his education had been better than that of most colonial boys, including Washington. To prepare for the examination, Henry had "boned up" on law from borrowed books.

The four law examiners, Randolph and Wythe, Robert Carter Nicholas and the elegant John Randolph, had not been exactly bowled over by this country bumpkin. And what a foursome for Henry to have to face. None was aware, of course, that their paths would cross many times in the future.

Disturbed by his rough appearance, John Randolph at first refused to examine Henry. But after a typically bad start, Henry revealed in his shrewd answers and solid reasoning the talent that was hidden beneath his back-country exterior. He seemed to grasp complicated law out of native intelligence.

Both John Randolph and Wythe signed his license—with misgivings—to practice in county and lower courts. George Dabney, a friend and kin of Henry's, later remarked, "I heard one of the Gentlemen who licensed him say that he was so ignorant of the law that he should not have passed him if he had not discovered his great genius."

Up to that time, Henry had seemed more interested in pleasures than anything else—in dancing jigs and reels, in playing the fiddle, which he did quite well, and in telling stories, which he also did well. Rather lazy and fond of idle talk, he had failed both as a farmer and as a storekeeper.

But then, early in the winter of 1763, after arguing minor cases in Hanover and adjoining counties, having to do mostly with matters of debt, Henry became involved in what appeared to be a hopeless litigation. He was attorney for the defense in a suit for back pay brought by the Anglican minister, the Reverend James Maury. It was an important case in that the Crown supported the Reverend Maury and the Anglican church was the official state church.

Henry was not known for much of anything, especially for public speaking. Only an hour before he got up to make his plea for the defense, he had told his uncle, for whom he had been named, the Reverend Patrick Henry, "You know that I have never yet spoken in public, and I fear I shall be too much overawed by your presence. . . ."

But soon the words began to flow. The country bumpkin was somehow transformed. He began to weave a magic spell and after a moment silence fell in the crowded room of Hanover Courthouse.

To make his points to the jurors, he used his body, his eyes, his hands. Those attending noted the dramatic pauses, the hypnotic way his voice "rose and fell." It was not the performance of an ordinary trial lawyer but the first electrifying moment when Patrick Henry soared in oratory. With it, he moved into areas of thought far beyond the now celebrated "Parson's Cause."

Astonishing words came forth from Henry, not the least of which were, "A king, by annulling or disallowing laws of this salutary nature, from being the father of his people degenerates into a tyrant and forfeits all rights to his subjects' obedience."

Henry was referring to the Crown's objection to a law passed by the General Assembly that fixed the amount and method of payment to Anglican ministers, and reduced the salaries of some. Although the churchmen were paid by the people in their parishes, or religious districts, the rates of payment, until the passage of this law, had been controlled by England.

In Henry's eyes, the case went beyond the matter of salaries. Henry was challenging British authority, questioning the right of the Crown to override the wishes of the colonial government.

Reportedly, murmurs of "treason" echoed in Hanover Courthouse when Henry finished his speech. But even if such accusations were not made, Henry had spoken strong words in opposition to the King's lawyer; he had unleashed a tongue that could drip honey or spray vinegar.

So, this third week of May, that much was definitely known about the solemn but amiable freshman burgess from the county of forests and gentle hills and babbling creeks that lay north of Richmond.

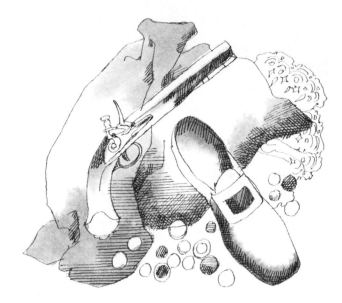

# 3 "If This Be Treason..."

Patrick Henry keeps a prudent but watchful silence during his first few days in the hall as numerous routine bills come up before the burgesses. They are of scant interest to him. One of them sets a bounty on wolves.

But on May 23rd a bill to establish a public loan office is introduced. It is Speaker Robinson's personal proposal and will grant loans to hard-pressed colony planters. Many are constantly in debt—land rich and cash poor. Henry rises to attack the bill, and the burgesses present are treated to their first brief but tantalizing sample of back-country oratory.

Thomas Jefferson, who is already interested in politics, is taking time off from his studies at the College of William and Mary to visit the session. He hears Henry ask, "What, sir, is it proposed, then, to reclaim the spendthrift from his dissipation and extravagance by filling his pockets with money?"

Speaker Robinson is plainly startled. His friends are also taking a long second look at the brash intruder. According to custom, this loblolly pine of a man should keep his rustic lips pursed; he should listen and learn from his elders. As a new burgess, his standing is low. The man has to be a fool, or insane, to call the revered planters "spendthrifts" and accuse them of "dissipation and extravagance," even though it might be true.

Henry is brushed aside and the measure predictably passes as conservative weight is displayed. It does, however, go down to defeat in the Council.

However, Henry is not aware, nor are most of the burgesses, that Speaker Robinson has lent large sums of treasury money to friends. He's also lent them a considerable amount of personal money.

Whether or not the public loan office was a scheme to help recoup his losses remains a question to this day. But Robinson's involvement was apparently not the reason for Henry's questioning of the bill. His frugal nature and a growing dislike of the conservatives caused him to balk at the idea. Aside from prompting Henry's first speech to the burgesses, the matter was of no importance until Robinson's loans were discovered upon his death.

Quickly overshadowing this political squabble is the word just received from England that the Stamp Act petitions of the past fall were not granted a hearing in London. The Stamp Act had passed in the House of Commons with little opposition and, almost with yawns, it had received the approval of the House of Lords. Then King George III added his royal signature. It was now *law.*

Henry is enraged as are other members of the House of Burgesses and later he makes known his feelings to such members as John Fleming of Cumberland County and Thomas Johnson of Louisa County. They discuss the matter, and decide, from the liberal, progressive view, what might be done.

The planning of business is such that the burgesses will not debate the stamp duties until the final two or three days of the four-week session. Many of the burgesses will have left Williamsburg by then to escape the growing humidity, and so the timing of the discussion is another indication of the colony's surrender to Parliament. The delegates feel little optimism that they can prevent England from collecting the tax.

On May 30, by previous plan with Henry, Thomas Johnson rises to propose that the House meet as a Committee of the Whole, a move enabling the burgesses to debate the Stamp Act without having to submit the discussion to record. The move is seconded.

Present are only thirty-nine of the sixty members and a handful of spectators, including, again, Thomas Jefferson. Speaker Robinson steps down from the dais and Peyton Randolph goes forward to assume chairmanship of the committee.

At this point, it seems obvious that the discussion will be little more than a tired, rather hopeless gesture of disagreement with the Crown. The petitions, most burgesses think, have already said almost everything that can be said.

Henry, twenty-nine years old, is one of the youngest burgesses in the hall. The bench on which he is seated is scarcely familiar with his backside after only nine days of occupancy. Yet he

again breaks with tradition and introduces five resolutions, written sometime during the past week.
They have all the fire of Wythe's original petitions; several are couched in even more pointed
language.

The first four resolutions claim that the people
of the colonies hold and enjoy the same rights and
liberties as the people of Great Britain; that the
taxation of the people by "themselves"—that is to
say, by their elected representatives—is a distin-
guishing characteristic of British freedom; that His
Majesty's people of "this most ancient colony have
uninterruptedly enjoyed the right of being governed by their own Assembly. . . ."

Then in his fifth resolution Henry throws a direct challenge at Parliament and the King:

> Resolved, therefore, that the General Assembly of this
> Colony have the sole Right and Power to lay Taxes and
> Impositions upon the inhabitants of this Colony; and
> that every Attempt to vest such power in any other Per-
> son or Persons whatsoever, other than the General As-
> sembly aforesaid, has a manifest Tendency to destroy
> British as well as American freedom.

Once again, within a period of two weeks, Mr.
Henry has stunned the House of Burgesses. No
Virginia legislator within memory has ever gone
this far in testing the Crown. In telling Parliament

it cannot lay taxes without the consent of the General Assembly, there is effrontery if not open rebellion. The conservatives gasp, having forgotten that their predecessors had made the same point a hundred and fifty years earlier.

It is one thing to petition London politely, to request aid or to complain about injustices, real or imagined; it is another matter, of far more gravity, to put the General Assembly of these times on firm record as claiming the sole right to tax the inhabitants of the colony.

The first four resolutions are carried by narrow margins, support coming largely from back-country burgesses, who, at last, may have a leader. The conservative old guard—Robinson, Peyton Randolph, Edmund Pendleton, Richard Bland, Robert Carter Nicholas, and even George Wythe—is in bitter opposition. Nicholas, the wealthy grandson of Robert Carter, "King Carter" as he was called, who owned 300,000 acres and 1,100 slaves when he died, is appalled.

Debate begins on the fifth resolution and Thomas Jefferson, standing in the doorway of the hall, describes it as "most bloody." Later, Henry is to recount, "Many threats were uttered and much abuse cast upon me."

Henry is attacked by men well versed in legislative debate. Thrown at him is the combined skill and knowledge of his peers, men who know how to use words both to persuade and destroy. But the Hanover lawyer proves to be as rugged as his clothing.

Legend has it that sometime during the debate, on this day or the next, Henry duels at his opposition with the words "Caesar had his Brutus, Charles the First his Cromwell, and George the Third . . ."

Brutus and Oliver Cromwell were the ruin of Caesar and Charles the First, and Henry was perhaps saying that George Grenville, the British chancellor of the exchequer, would bring about the downfall of King George.

Robinson is then supposed to have shouted, "Treason! Treason!"

Several accounts say that Mr. Henry stood in cool disregard until the hall was quiet enough for him to finish. And then, it is claimed, he went on:

". . . George the Third may profit by their example. If this be treason, make the most of it."

Other accounts, particularly one from a French traveler, offer much tamer and probably more accurate versions of this speech. According to the Frenchman's notes, Henry apologized if his words

were construed to be treasonable. It is possible that Henry himself made no reference to "treason."

Whatever Patrick Henry said this hot May day, when the record of debate was not kept, all the past words about the rights of the American colonists had been eclipsed. It was both what he said and how he said it. The spirit of defiance, bursting out in a colonial legislative hall, was significant.

After additional debate, the fifth resolution is reread; then read twice again. With some amending, it also passes by a thin margin, the back-country burgesses again providing the bulk of support. An angry Robinson returns to the dais to resume his chair and the Committee of the Whole is dismissed.

Edmund Pendleton, with deep loyalties to the Crown, is naturally dismayed, as are all of his conservative colleagues. A swearing Peyton Randolph sweeps angrily through the door past Jefferson. In transit, he exclaims he would have "given a hundred guineas for a single vote."

Patrick Henry does not tarry long. Perhaps he shops a bit on this afternoon for his wife, Sarah, and their six children. He has found modest prosperity in his law practice and the family is soon to move into a new house on Roundabout Creek in Louisa County.

There are many excellent shops along Duke of Gloucester Street and the side streets. There is Prentis & Company, Holt's, and Greenhow's, all general stores; Geddy, the silversmith; Hay, the cabinetmaker; Pasteur's apothecary shop. Guns, silks, satins, laces, buttons, china, hats, shoes, clocks, candy—much that makes life pleasant can be obtained in Williamsburg. Items that cannot be obtained in Williamsburg, or Richmond, are ordered from London, but it takes many months for the sailing ships to travel to and return from England.

One source claims that an unperturbed Henry was seen leaving town "along Duke of Gloucester Street . . . wearing buckskin breeches, leading a lean horse and chatting with Paul Carrington," another burgess.

While this may be a romantic picture of the triumphant newcomer, especially the part about the buckskin breeches, which usually were worn only when riding in rough country, it is the only available glimpse we have of him on this afternoon.

The next day, Saturday, the burgesses who are still in town meet in a final session. By now, Governor Francis Fauquier knows of the resolutions and one of his Council members, Colonel Peter Randolph, spends some time Saturday morning

searching for legal precedents to expunge, or remove, that appalling—in the minds of the conservatives—fifth resolution.

Soon after the burgesses are called to order, the
ruling clique does strike out the fifth resolve. But
they cannot erase the insolent words spoken by
Henry in the hall of the House of Burgesses nor
can they prevent copies of the original set of resolutions from circulating in Williamsburg and away
from it.

A shaken Governor Fauquier then exercises the
Crown's authority to dissolve the General Assembly for the spring session. Williamsburg settles
down to face the usual moist heat of summer in
Tidewater Virginia.

# 4  The Capital

Richmond, to the west, is a smaller town, and Norfolk, the busy seaport to the south at the entrance to Chesapeake Bay, is much larger, but Williamsburg has its own special fame. It is the seat of government. Appointed by the King, the British lieutenant governor, though always addressed as governor, resides here; the high courts meet here in addition to the General Assembly. There is also the College of William and Mary to distinguish the town.

As far back as 1693, when the colony was about eighty years old, a university had been chartered at Middle Plantation, between the James and York rivers. The site was then described as a place with "temperate aire dry and champaign land and plentifully stored with Wholsom Springs." The decision to make the site the capital of Virginia came in May, 1699, and the following month the "city" of Williamsburg was founded, named after England's King William.

So, as June, 1765, arrives, the capital is a bit more than sixty-five years old. Severe thunderstorms sometimes hit the Tidewater and many of the brick and white-painted wooden buildings, even the first college building and the Capitol, were struck by lightning and destroyed by fire; they have now been rebuilt. Fire is a constant hazard, and chains of men with buckets of creek water can do little to stop the flames.

But the quiet setting on a low ridge in gently rolling plantation country, where tobacco, corn, and livestock thrive, is deceptive. In its own way, Williamsburg is pulsing and dynamic, full of life and laughter.

Approximately a thousand black and white residents live in the seat of colonial rule, catering to the needs of travelers, be they burgesses from distant counties or foreigners passing through. Williamsburg, administered by a mayor and his aldermen, is not a seaport and is totally lacking in industry. There are tinners and blacksmiths and candlemakers and wigmakers and makers of harness and snuff, soap-boilers, goldsmiths, and dancing masters, but the product the town boasts about is politics. And with the likes of Peyton Randolph, George Wythe, Richard Henry Lee, and that former surveyor George Washington frequently in residence, Williamsburg can hold up its head with Boston and Philadelphia, not to mention New York.

Over the town's more than two hundred acres are spread residences, both humble and grand, the buildings of government, and many shops and inns, comfortably spaced. Even in normal times, when the politicians have gone home and the courts are not in session, elegant carriages—for there is great wealth in Virginia—jangle along the sandy streets. Men on horseback, in dress varying from white-wigged dandy to farmer homespun and frontier buckskin, plod in for business or pleasure or to talk politics.

At one end of the oblong town, amidst trees, loom the three brick buildings of the College of William and Mary, fronted by a grassy courtyard with gravel walks. The James and York rivers, three miles away, can be seen from the roof of the main building on clear days.

At the opposite end of town, more than a mile away, is the Capitol, a rather large and commanding two-storied brick building, made in the shape of an H and set behind a brick wall. It is easily visible from the college courtyard.

Sandy Duke of Gloucester Street, very wide for its time, connects the two areas, providing the pleasant, tree-lined heart of town. Going up Duke of Gloucester from the college, just past Bruton Parish Church, visitors can look north toward the imposing Palace Green; beyond it stands the Governor's Palace, current home of the gentle, scholarly Francis Fauquier.

Busy Market Square and the James County Courthouse are midway between the college and the Capitol, with the octagonal brick Powder Magazine standing in the clear nearby. One day the Powder Magazine will become the symbol of the colony's defiance of the King and Parliament.

Continuing along Duke of Gloucester toward the Capitol, visitors come to a solid group of buildings on either side of the street. They are mostly inns, also called ordinaries, taverns, and shops. One of the buildings, the Raleigh, is *the* tavern. So famous is it that businessmen such as saddlers and wigmakers advertise their places of commerce as "being near the Raleigh." British governors often entertain there. George Washington and the student Thomas Jefferson know it well. But so does every boy and girl in town.

The food is generally good at the inns but the drinking water is awful, which is one reason why a fair amount of wine, ale, cider, and grog is consumed. The sleeping arrangements leave something to be desired—six to eight men in a small room during busy seasons.

The Capitol, with British flag flying impressively above, is, of course, an improvement on the one destroyed by fire. A February 5, 1747, dispatch was sent by rider to the *Pennsylvania Gazette* in Philadelphia and printed in the April 2nd issue. News did not travel very fast.

> Last Friday (January 30) the fatal and ever memorable Day of the Martyrdom of King Charles, the First, a most extraordinary Misfortune befel this place, by the destruction of our fine Capitol. Between 7 and 8 o'clock in the morning, the inhabitants of this city were surprised with the sight of Smoak, issuing from the upper part . . .

Some people suggested arsonists were responsible for the fire. The town is not without criminals. Often, the Public Gaol, or jail, is occupied. Occasionally, convicted citizens, male or female, could be seen sitting in the stocks in the gaol yard. Sometimes, bodies swing from the gallows. A few of Blackbeard's "pyrates" had been hanged in Williamsburg years earlier.

In the new Capitol building the General Court and the meeting hall for the burgesses are on the first floor along with the clerk's offices. On the second floor are the committee rooms and the cham-

ber of the Council, lined with lawbooks, with the governor's chair at the head of the conference table. Decorations inside the building, including portraits of past royalty, and ornaments over the main iron gate outside, in the form of carved and gilded King's Arms, pay homage to the distant Crown.

Behind the Capitol is the Exchange, a green area, an informal, noisy place for commerce. Weather permitting, men of all trades and professions, from sea captains to plantation owners, meet on the grass to buy and sell.

mp

Nearby is the theater, well attended for almost any event, and not far away is the racetrack to satisfy the love of fast horses and hard wagering—a love that all Virginians seem to share, landed gentry, simple tradesmen, and slaves alike.

During the period called "Publick Times," when the General Court is convened, and also during the sessions of the General Assembly, the town takes on a hearty, unmannered carnival atmosphere. Beginning in late morning, the streets bustle and throb as a steady stream of traffic goes to and from the Capitol, the wheels of the carriages stirring up dust on dry days and spinning in sandy slosh on wet ones. The mood, often raucous, lasts until late at night when the clink of glasses and bursts of laughter finally fade away.

The gentry parade to and from the festivities in carriages and coaches—the ladies in silk finery, the silver-buckled men in spotless white stockings, velvet breeches, brocaded coats, and tricornered hats. There are barbecues, private parties, sumptuous dinners, and great balls, as well as performances and lectures at the theater. Those who are so inclined can watch dramas or magicians, laugh at comedians or listen to chamber music. Shakespeare's plays are favorites in Williamsburg, but one can also hear an oration on the art of sneezing. In other parts of town more earthy entertainment is offered in the form of cockfights and boxing and wrestling matches.

Canny local craftsmen always wait until these periods of the year to display their best wares, the merchants putting out the latest silk fashions from London. A rather different enterprise that takes place in these weeks is the local slave auction, drawing many planters from the area.

It is said that everyone who is anyone and many who are "purely nothing" come to Williamsburg during the Publick Times.

Of course, the town settles down after December when it can become chattering cold in the Tidewater area, cold enough even to freeze the nearby ponds for ice-skating. Much visiting takes place then, and tables creak with food, partaken with liberal amounts of good Madeira wine, one of the items soon to be taxed.

In comparison to sophisticated Philadelphia or worldly, commercial New York, Williamsburg is perhaps a humble place and in the estimation of some perfumed visitors from the north, or from across the sea, still a rough frontier town. In several ways, their judgment is accurate. Even young Tom Jefferson sometimes jokingly refers to it as "Devilsburg."

# 5 "Let's Rush In"

By the middle of the second week of June, 1765, Patrick Henry's "Caesar and Brutus" speech and his resolutions are topics of discussion throughout Virginia. A few people even gather in Williamsburg with the intent of "burning in effigy" the British chancellor of the exchequer, Lord Grenville, who had proposed the Stamp Act. At the same time, copies of the resolutions, in more or less their original form, are traveling north.

Two other resolutions, thought to be mainly the work of John Fleming, a burgess who agreed with Henry's ideas on the Stamp Act, did not reach a vote in the Assembly but were nevertheless included in these dispatches. The additional resolves claim that the "people are not bound to yield obedience to *any* law" except those passed by the Virginia Assembly; and that any person who maintains that the Assembly does not have the sole right to lay taxation on the people "shall be deemed an enemy to His Majesty's colony."

Strong words, these, piled on Mr. Henry's.

Copies of the resolutions—including the fifth resolve, which the burgesses had at the last minute erased—were smuggled out of the colony by Virginia liberals. They reach Philadelphia first, then New York; finally, as postriders, pouches full, pound along the road toward Boston, the flammatory resolves also arrive in New England.

In New York, however, a loyalist, or Tory, stronghold full of merchants devoted to the Crown, the resolves aren't printed. And even in Williamsburg the conservative editor of the *Virginia Gazette*, John Royle, refuses to print them. The resolves are published first in Rhode Island in the *Newport Mercury* on June 24, 1765. On July 1, they appear in the *Boston Gazette* with the comment, "The people of Virginia have spoken very sensibly, and the frozen politicians of a more northern Government say they have spoken Treason. . . ."

The prominent New Englander Oxenbridge Thacher, on his deathbed, said, "Oh, those Virginians are men; they are noble spirits."

Yes, there is a kindred spirit of rebellion in the north, particularly in Massachusetts Colony, the home of John Adams and his radical cousin, Sam Adams; John Hancock, the merchant; and the silversmith patriot Paul Revere. Of all the colonies, Virginia and Massachusetts have a reputation for jealously guarding the rights of the colonists.

The Massachusetts Assembly soon passes a resolution calling for all thirteen assemblies to meet in an "intercolonial congress" to debate the Stamp Act. In the past, the colonies have usually gone their separate ways in dealing with any problems with the Crown.

New Hampshire declines to attend the congress, and the governors of Virginia, North Carolina, and Georgia refuse to allow the colonial assemblies to reconvene to elect delegates to such an impertinent meeting. Delaware and New Jersey face similar treatment from their governors, but nevertheless elect delegates in informal sessions. South Carolina firmly commits herself to the congress. Rhode Island follows in late August, then Pennsylvania, Maryland, and Connecticut.

Ignited in Virginia by Mr. Henry, who is now branded a reckless radical, the protest goes beyond the often mild and gentlemanly legislative bodies of the colonies. Soon General Thomas Gage, the British military commander in New York, writes home that the Williamsburg resolutions have caused an "outcry" in the colonies.

Most important, though, is that the colonies are showing signs of uniting at last. The Henry-Fleming resolutions have acted both to inflame protests and spur unity.

In Boston the protests are taking an ugly turn. Earlier, in the late spring, probably even before Henry's roiling of the colonial waters, a group called the Loyal Nine was organized. They are shopkeepers and craftsmen for the most part, not openly connected with such political militants as John and Sam Adams.

In mid-August, gathering a mob, the Loyal Nine hangs in effigy one Andrew Oliver, the designated Distributor of Tax Stamps for Massachusetts. They march on the Town House, where the

Council is meeting, and then proceed to attack Oliver's house, even threatening to kill him. He soon resigns.

Some ten days later the Loyal Nine strikes again; this time their target is the house of Customs Collector Hallowell. Then they turn their wrath on the house of Lieutenant Governor Thomas Hutchinson, who had personally attempted to disperse them as they ripped up Oliver's residence.

Boston is frightened by the mob action and the militia is called out. Responsible men criticize the raid on the lieutenant governor's home but the Loyal Nine remains in business. They assume a new name, the Sons of Liberty. Similar organizations begin to operate in other colonies. Whatever their titles, the groups are, quite simply, revolutionary in aim.

Although accounts of violence make for the best talk in taverns, other means of protest are also being discussed throughout the colonies. Boycotts of British goods are proposed. Should the colonies cease to buy products made in England, Britain's merchants would be the first to complain to the Crown.

It is too simple to say that what is happening is due only to the Stamp Act. Socially, the colonies are growing up. Their populations are increasing. As more and more people are born in America, ties and loyalties to England automatically weaken. To many, England seems very far away. America is home. Yet few colonists, at this date, want "home rule" and its tremendous responsibilities. It is a restless, confusing time.

By fall, 1765, Williamsburg, where the initial flame was kindled by Mr. Henry, is in no less an angry mood than Boston. On Wednesday, October 30th, Colonel George Mercer returns from England to take up duty with his batch of new tax stamps, effective November 1st.

If the colonel, on approaching Williamsburg, is somewhat edgy about his new job, he has ample reason to be. On debarking from his sailing vessel in the port of Hampton, he was almost mobbed by angry citizens. By now, he has also heard that he was hung in effigy in Virginia's Westmoreland County. But the men appointed to collect the stamp tax are in trouble everywhere. Annapolis, Maryland, has hanged its collector in effigy, too.

Mild-mannered Governor Fauquier, who spends much of his time reading or enjoying card games with friends, is concerned for the safety of Mercer and, along with Speaker Robinson and several Council members, goes out to meet him. A crowd has already gathered at the Exchange, near the Capitol, and the first words Fauquier hears are somewhat disquieting: "One and all." The crowd seems to be planning some kind of united action, perhaps violent.

The mob, as Fauquier describes it, then heads for Mrs. Campbell's coffeehouse, which faces the Exchange on Waller Street, but happens on the unfortunate colonel, who is on his way to the Capitol. Plainly, this is not a collection of riffraff from Cumberland and Hanover counties. Rather, some of Williamsburg's best-known merchants, along with a number of planters, are facing the uneasy Mercer. They demand to know whether or not he'll resign. Mercer tactfully replies that he has to have time to think it over and promises an answer on Friday, the very day the tax is to begin. Deciding against continuing to the Capitol, Mercer heads for the coffeehouse. The crowd follows, not at all satisfied with his reply.

Governor Fauquier seats himself on Mrs. Campbell's wide porch, with Robinson and other Council members acting as a barrier to the crowd. The protesters remain quiet enough while the governor greets Mercer, but to "judge their Countenances they were not well pleased," Fauquier later writes. "Now and then a voice was heard from the Crowd that Friday was too late . . . after some time, a Cry was heard, 'Let's rush in' . . ."

Exactly how long the confrontation lasts is not known, but Governor Fauquier later writes to London: "It was growing dark and I did not think it safe to leave Mr. Mercer behind me, so I again advanced to the Edge of the Steps and said aloud I believed no man there would do me Hurt, and turned to Mercer & told him that if he would walk with me through the People I believed I could conduct him safe to my house . . ."

Colonel Mercer resigns the next day and not a single stamp is ever issued in Virginia Colony.

A Stamp Act Congress meets in New York in October, with nine colonies represented, and manages to draft a resolution. Drawing from Henry's resolves and those of other colonial assemblies, the wording falls short of any direct threat to the Crown. However, the congress's resolution does represent an almost unified protest. Even New Hampshire, which had declined to attend the congress, gives approval to the resolution. Furthermore, the congress represents the first attempt in recent history to bring the colonial leaders together. As early as 1684, a meeting had been held between representatives of Virginia, Massachusetts, and New York to discuss affairs of mutual interest. But such meetings were few. The links between the colonies had always been weak.

Governor Fauquier, wisely for the King's sake, has decided not to convene the General Assembly this fall; he was not about to deliver up another chance for debate of the Stamp Act and provide Patrick Henry with another opportunity to take a swipe at the Crown.

Mr. Henry is at home, taking care of his law practice, sometimes riding a hundred miles to argue a single case. The family is now in residence in the new house on Roundabout Creek. His views about another possibly disastrous bill passed by Parliament this year are not known. Called the Quartering Act, it will require that the colonies house, feed, and transport British officers and soldiers. Houses, inns, barns, and other buildings will be given to the troops; the colonists will have to haul the soldiers about in wagons. Furthermore, additional military units will be sent from England to enforce British laws. At any other time, the measure would have aroused fury but in the tempest over the Stamp Act it is almost unnoticed.

Meanwhile, Richard Henry Lee, son of the distinguished Council member Thomas Lee, but more allied with Henry's thinking than with his father's, has made a bad mistake and is now attempting to rectify it. In the months prior to Henry's speech and the general outcry, Lee had made application for a post as a collector of stamp taxes. There is no better patriot in any colony than the tall and witty R. H. Lee, and he will soon be branded a radical, too. But now, in February, 1766, he is trying to erase his foolish political move by organizing an "association" in Westmoreland County to boycott all British goods until the Stamp Act is repealed.

Coupled with the suddenly belligerent mood of the colonies, the boycotts, now rapidly spreading, affect England economically. They alone put teeth into whatever news of colonial discontent is printed in London and Edinburgh. And the Sons of Liberty have now sprouted in Virginia. Loosely knit, these groups of patriots can make themselves felt when a Tory merchant decides to cooperate with the Crown by ignoring the boycotts. The Sons of Liberty are quite capable of tossing London-labeled goods into muddy streets.

Finally, a combination of protests from the colonies and from disturbed merchants in England and Scotland force abandonment of the hated Stamp Act. On March 18, 1766, King George reluctantly signs the bill for total repeal, and three months later Governor Fauquier issues a proclamation announcing termination of the act.

Eleven days later, the *Virginia Gazette* prints:

> On Friday last . . . upon the joyful Occasion of the Repeal of the Stamp Act and the universal Pleasure and Satisfaction it gives that all Differences between the Mother Country and her Colonies are happily terminated, was manifested here by General Illuminations and a Ball and Elegant Entertainments at the Capitol, at which was present his Honour the Governor, many members of His Majesty's Council, and a large and genteel Company of Ladies and Gentlemen, who spent an Evening with much Mirth and Decorum, and drank all the loyal and patriotick Toasts . . .

All differences "happily terminated"? Not quite. Parliament has passed the Declaratory Act this year. It says, very clearly, that Parliament is supreme in making laws for the colonies. Those who think that Parliament cannot and will not tax the colonies are dreamers.

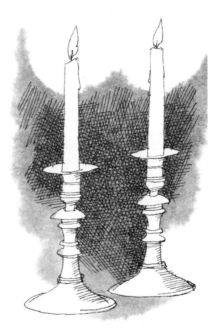

# 6 The Good Baron de Botetourt

A year and a few months of comparative harmony pass, but the Stamp Act is hardly forgotten. More than any other issue in the history of the colonies, it has served to unify the people, to cement, in particular, relations between those two potential political volcanoes, Massachusetts and Virginia. Though they haven't yet met Patrick Henry, the

49

Adamses and John Hancock in Boston know that in him, and others in Virginia, they have ready and willing allies. The colonies will present a more united front in their future dealings with the Crown.

Meanwhile, in England, the great statesman William Pitt, a man usually sympathetic to the colonies, is in decline because of ill health and is unable to cope with the new chancellor of the exchequer, Charles Townshend. With little affection for the colonies, Townshend, soon to become a court favorite of George III, goes about undoing the shaky peace.

To the House of Commons, Townshend announces, "I know a Mode by which a Revenue may be drawn from America without offense. . . . I laugh at the distinction between internal and external Taxation."

In reality, there is little distinction. Taxes are taxes. Some are direct; others are largely invisible and indirect, paid at the customhouse. Under any name, customs are still taxes. England had failed in her attempt to tax the colonies directly under the Stamp Act; now taxes would be indirect, in the form of import duties paid on British products.

Looking up to the galleries where colonial agents, men who represented and monitored Parliament for the colonies—lobbyists in a way—usually sat, Townshend said, "I speak this aloud, that you who are in the galleries may hear; and after this, I do not expect to have my statue erected in America." He realized he would be hated.

Sitting down, the brooding man added, "England is undone if this Taxation of America is given up." Presumably, he meant that if England abandoned the right to tax the colonies, she would eventually lose control of them.

In his proposed legislation, duties, which were to be collected at American ports, were imposed on lead, paper, paint, glass, and tea, all British exports. In addition, commissioners were to be established in America to make certain the duties were collected. The measures were passed by Parliament in the spring of 1767.

For the colonists, the new laws mark a weary return to the Stamp Act and the issues it raised. Great Britain has already declared its supreme right to impose the new taxes without the consent of the colonial assemblies, and though few people in the colonies would have agreed, probably did have the right, by constitution, to enforce the Stamp Act.

In the spring of 1768, following the death of Governor Fauquier, whom the citizens of Williamsburg mourned as a warm and moderate leader, the House of Burgesses reacts to Townshend's laws with a protest drawn up by Richard Bland, who is by no means a hothead.

Little has changed. The Crown and the colonies are on collision course again. The presence of British troops in various colonies, supposedly for the purpose of defense but also to quell uprising, adds to the unrest. They have been arriving since early 1767. When New York refused to house and feed them, Parliament responded by suspending the New York General Assembly.

The fires of rebellion grow slowly, but steadily.

On October 27, 1768, the *Virginia Gazette* printed:

> Last Tuesday evening, arrived in Hampton Roads, in eight weeks from Portsmouth, the Rippon Man O' War of 60 guns . . . having on board the Right Honourable Norbourne Berkeley, the Baron de Botetourt. His Majesty's Lieutenant and Governor General of this Colony and Dominion . . .

For the first time since the late seventeenth century, Virginia is to have a resident governor. Past lieutenant governors, though always addressed as "governor," had been representatives of the appointed governor general who remained in England, doing little to deserve his "court plum" job.

Botetourt's arrival is a happy one for that reason and others. He is a nobleman, which appeals to Virginia aristocrat and commoner alike. A bachelor, he reportedly has a fondness for gambling, an item in his favor as far as certain gentry are concerned. All in all, he is estimated to be a personable man who might make a fine governor.

After a ride in the state coach from Hampton, he is met with appropriate fanfare, sworn in, and then proceeds to supper at the Raleigh Tavern with the Council members, while outside, the city is "illuminated." High honors, indeed, are the Grand Illuminations. Candles flicker in the Capitol and in the windows of inns, shops, and houses, casting warm welcoming glows. The town is in a mood for gaiety; the taverns are crowded and noisy.

Soon Botetourt writes London: "I have been asked every day to Dinner by the principal Gentlemen, and am at present upon the very best terms with all. . . ." It is a correct appraisal. Immediately, he is well liked. He begins repaying his hosts with fine dinners at the palace, either in the supper room or in the formal dining room, where sixty can be seated.

In the period between Fauquier's death and the baron's splendorous arrival, Williamsburg's residents went about their ways with little mention of the soon-to-be-imposed Townshend tariffs. It was another one of those times of calm, as if the town, enjoying itself, were taking a holiday from strife and argument.

Mr. Henry said little during these months, and the bell at Bruton Parish Church tolled only in peace, never to summon the people for protest. Organist Peter Pelham, who is also the jailer, plays for Sunday services, weddings, and funerals. The new organ is a proud addition to the church, which is usually filled on the Sabbath. Religion is deeply ingrained in the people of Williamsburg.

On April 11, 1768, when the spring fair trotted out its agricultural exhibits and "animal wonders," young Thomas Jefferson, having finished his education and having procured a license to practice law, paid 7½ pence to see an "elk," a beast not common to the Tidewater. At about the same time, he attended the opening performance of *The Honest Yorkshireman*, the new play at the local theater.

On May 2nd, George Washington joined Jefferson in the audience for still another presentation. The repertory was offering a good selection that season, everything from dance to drama. Even a ballad opera had been performed. Jefferson, of course, had a great interest in the theater and even more in music. He played the violin. There was considerable culture in the town he jokingly called "Devilsburg."

Summer, fall, and winter slid peacefully by and spring returned to Virginia with its usual display of dogwood and wild cherry blossoms and fragrant jasmine; another fair, another theatrical season. This time, magicians and puppeteers are the attractions. To usher in the season, Jefferson attends the puppet performance of *Babes in the Woods* on April 14th, with the cast "richly dressed, four feet high."

On the same bill is a spectacle advertised as a "curious view of Water Works, representing the sea, with all manner of sea monsters snorting on the waves." There are indoor fireworks and for the finale a performer lays his head on "one chair and his feet on another and suffered a large rock of three hundred weight to be broken on his chest with a sledge hammer."

It was a curtain raiser for another spectacle that occurs the following month. On May 8th, Governor Botetourt convenes the General Assembly. To the ceremonies, the governor wears an elaborate coat of gold thread and rides to the Capitol in a coach drawn by six white horses. Emblazoned on the side of the coach is the Virginia coat of arms rather than the royal symbol. Williamsburg has never seen anything like it and much approves.

Although some conservative members have been voted out of office, possibly because of their opposition to the Stamp Act resolves, the notable faces are back again, including Henry's dark wedge. Among the new members is a freckle-faced young man from Albemarle County, the same young man who used to sit on the steps of Nancy Blair's house on Duke of Gloucester Street, harmonizing on deepening spring evenings. Thomas Jefferson is largely in agreement with Patrick Henry at this point in his career. His brand of politics is progressive.

The burgesses settle down to work and inevitably they will tackle the Townshend acts. They must also deal with a new threat from Parliament: the right to try American colonists in England for treason and felonies. Such offenses had previously been tried in America. It is not difficult to envision Patrick Henry or John Fleming or R. H. Lee pondering a trip across the Atlantic in chains, eating swill, a stay in London Tower prison, and a dangle from the gallows on nearby Tower Hill.

A few days after the opening of the session, John Blair reports out of the Committee of the Whole with four resolves that challenge Parliament. Patrick Henry and Richard Henry Lee have had a hand in their preparation. The first resolve, against the Townshend tariffs, again flatly states that only the burgesses can impose a tax on the people of Virginia. The measure carries without great opposition. The liberals are pleased.

The next day, Baron Botetourt, perhaps reluctantly, because he is already in sympathy with the Virginians, dismisses the Assembly as a hint of official disapproval. However, the burgesses do not stay dissolved. For the first time in their long history, they decide to meet without government authority, retiring to the Apollo Room of the Raleigh Tavern. Peyton Randolph, speaker of the house since John Robinson's death, is again elected to that office.

The meeting begins. What is now taking place in the Raleigh is in clear contempt of the Crown and no legislation can be voted on. So other matters are debated. During the protests of the Stamp Act, one of the most effective actions was the boycott of British goods. They discuss this once again after George Washington presents a masterful paper from the skilled pen of his neighbor, George Mason, of Gunston Hall plantation.

Acting now as concerned citizens more than legislators, they adopt a Non-Importation Agreement on slaves, wines, and British dry goods. Peyton

Randolph, so bitterly opposed to Patrick Henry four years previously, now leads the way. Further, it is proposed that an association be formed between the burgesses and the leading merchants of the colony to add power to the agreement. Boycotting could be enforced more easily as the result of such an agreement.

The threat of a boycott, from Virginia and other colonies, reaches England during the summer and appears to obtain the desired results. At the November session of the General Assembly, Governor Botetourt tells the burgesses that he has word that the present Parliament won't lay "further Taxes upon America for the purpose of raising Revenue," and that there would be proposals at the next session to "take Duties off Glass, Paper and Colours . . ." Later Botetourt even goes to the extent of claiming he will ask to be recalled if the "obnoxious Townshend tariffs" are not repealed— little wonder he is popular in Williamsburg.

But at the high-fashion December ball, when the speaker and burgesses entertain the governor at the Capitol, the ladies of the area make their own silent points about the "obnoxious" levies by attending in homespun rather than in their usual lavish, imported gowns. The sight of the buxom grand ladies swirling in peasant cloth would be enough to convince any governor of unhappiness within his domain.

But 'tis Christmas in Williamsburg, days to forget about the rascal Charles Townshend and celebrate. Carolers singing "God Rest Ye Merry, Gentlemen" are out in the crisp cold, their lanthorns held high. Kitchens are in a state of siege with prime Virginia ham, roast beef, wild turkey, pheasant, and oysters fighting for table space with cherry tarts and fruitcakes. Punch, cider, Madeira wine, and Jamaica rum will flow to wash it all down.

Christmas Day is set aside to worship at Bruton Parish Church, and then feast. Feast for the next "Twelve Days" of Christmas. On New Year's Day, some children will get gifts of books or gloves. There are decorations in homes and shops; cannon and musket firing will salute the season.

By January 6th, which marks the end of the Christmas season in England and the colonies, Williamsburg is a weary and well-fed town.

# 7 The Pot Boils Over

In the eyes of official London, the people of Boston, if not the people of all Massachusetts Bay Colony, are apt to be troublemakers. It is true that Bostonians appear to be more stubborn and short-tempered than most of the other colonists. It is also true that they are seldom reluctant to show their feelings.

Simmering hatred over the stationing of two British regiments in Boston flares on the night of March 5, 1770. The trouble begins when a few boys snowball a British customhouse sentry. Six Redcoats, under command of Captain Thomas Preston, come to his aid. In minutes, about sixty men and boys, reportedly led by black patriot Crispus Attucks, are involved. Heated words are exchanged; stones begin to fly toward the soldiers. An eyewitness later testifies that Attucks brandishes a stick. Whatever the true circumstance, gunfire sounds on King Street and three of the patriots, including Attucks, die instantly; two more are mortally wounded.

News of the incident, termed the "Boston Massacre," sweeps into the other colonies and the fact that the soldiers were somewhat provoked is overlooked. Colonists everywhere are angry and sharp resentment toward Great Britain is once again stirred.

In Williamsburg, however, the summer passes calmly enough. But in the fall an unexpected event marks the beginning of change. On Friday, October 19, a funeral procession, led by muffled drums beating through black cloth, begins at the Governor's Palace and moves slowly up the green, past the Everard House and George Wythe's and Elka-

nah Deane's, toward Duke of Gloucester Street, finally to stop outside the brick wall of Bruton Church. The bell rings sadly this day.

Services are held for Norborne Berkeley, the Baron de Botetourt, dead after a short illness. He will long be remembered as a kindly leader and friend. He is buried at the college.

Almost another year passes before the dusty royal coach of the new chief executive, John Murray, Earl of Dunmore, rolls through the gates of the palace. He is accompanied by his secretary, Captain Foy. Lady Dunmore and the children are in England.

It is too much to expect that this new resident will have the warmth or wisdom of a Fauquier or a Botetourt. A rather stocky man, he appears to be slightly arrogant. Not a great deal is known about him except that he is Scottish. As a number of Scots have immigrated to the colony, Virginia knows firsthand that they can be prickly and as stubborn as oak heart.

Dunmore's first experience with the General Assembly comes the following spring, but the session is unimportant so far as new legislation and resolutions are concerned. There are no clashes. However, as the months go by, it becomes quite apparent that his lordship tends to be a difficult man. He refuses, for a while, to keep office hours. Furthermore, he does not call another Assembly until March, 1773, and then only because counterfeiters are at work in the colony, duplicating pound notes. He wants the legislators to do something about the criminal element.

This time, though, there is another intriguing political situation to occupy the burgesses. A special Court of Inquiry has been established by the Crown in Rhode Island with the power to send accused persons out of the colony for trial, the legality of which had been questioned before by Henry and others. The specter of facing a magistrate in London instead of a local jury looms again and, foreseeing its implications, the dissidents react.

Jefferson wrote, "Not thinking our old and leading members up to the point of Forwardness and Zeal which the times required, Mr. Henry, Richard Henry Lee, Francis Lightfoot Lee and myself agreed to meet in the evening in a private room in the Raleigh Tavern to consult on the State of Things."

Out of that evening's secret talk came a resolution to establish a Committee on Correspondence among all the colonies, really a "civilian intelligence bureau," the first to operate in America. It is the idea of Richard Henry Lee, whose earlier boycott scheme for Virginia had worked so well.

On matters such as the special court in Rhode Island, arising from the 1772 burning by New England colonists of a British schooner which was hunting for tea smugglers, the colonies will now "exchange" information by letters. They will brief each other on problems of mutual interest and alert each other on courses of action that they plan to take. The measure passes the house easily, progressives and conservatives uniting.

Suddenly, on March 15th, only ten days into the session, Lord Dunmore calls a halt to the meetings at the Capitol. The decision to set up an "intelligence bureau," soon to operate under Dunmore's nose, seemingly has nothing to do with his decision, however. In fact, why he did dissolve the Assembly was a mystery. Nonetheless, the burgesses go home, their annoyance increased by his high-handed treatment.

The vote to establish a Committee on Correspondence reflects a new attitude on the part of the burgesses. They feel now that whatever troubles Rhode Island, Boston, or Charleston will eventually also trouble Williamsburg. The colonies, growing steadily, reaching toward a population of three million, will never again be loosely connected wilderness settlements having little in common except an overseas royal government.

For instance, trouble over the tax on tea has been brewing for years. Because of boycotts in the colonies and agitation from London merchants, most of the Townshend tariffs are but an unpleasant memory. The notable and chafing exception is the tariff on tea. The average transplanted Englishman, or even native-born colonist, could happily do without many things but not without tea. Tea had long been considered a household necessity, not a luxury. To avoid the Townshend duties, many colonists had been buying East India leaf smuggled in by Dutch ships. It was cheaper and tasted just as good as the British brands.

Over the past months there have been persistent rumors that large consignments of tea are to be shipped from Great Britain. They will be entered with the British export duty removed but the special Townshend tariff retained. Warning letters arrived during the summer, after Parliament amended the Tea Act.

Now, in this fall of 1773, the news is confirmed. Six hundred thousand pounds of prime leaf, property of the powerful but financially strapped British East India Company, will be introduced into the colonies in early winter. The tea is in London warehouses and, likely, at least one cargo is already underway.

Merchants, patriots, even smugglers, all for their own reasons, take an interest. With the export duty—the fee paid in London by the shipper —removed, the tea will be cheaper, undercutting colonial merchants who already have stocks of tea on which both export and import duties have been paid. Furthermore, by accepting the shipments, the colonists will in effect be recognizing the loathsome special Townshend tariff.

A need for quick protest is indicated. Letters appear in New York, Philadelphia, and Boston newspapers, written by both patriots and merchants, threatening to "tar and feather" anyone caught dealing with the shipments.

In Boston, John Hancock, who is never too busy as a merchant to tackle political issues, and ever-ready Samuel Adams, among others, immediately see an opportunity to relight the fires of resistance. For three years the colonies have been too quiet and passive, they think. Sam Adams fears that the colonists will become so lamblike they'll never come to grips with the Crown. Adams and Hancock decide to take a stand.

The first tea carrier, the vessel *Dartmouth*, with

114 chests of excellent East India aboard, angles into Boston harbor on a gray Sunday afternoon, November 28th. It drops sails and anchors while patriot sentinels watch. The arrival of the ship is hardly a surprise.

For more than a month, with the local merchants, the intended importers, subjected to constant threats to life and limb, Lieutenant Governor Thomas Hutchinson has been trying to figure out a way to land the tea, have it taxed, and still keep the peace. The memory of threats to his own life and the destruction of his house during the Stamp Act crisis have not faded. The people of Boston have on occasion been far from lamblike.

# 8 "An Epoch in History"

Monday morning, November 29th, the bells of Boston ring out and citizens head toward Faneuil Hall. They'd read the posted notices saying, "Friends! Brethren! Countrymen! The Hour of Destruction of Manly Opposition to the Machinations of Tyranny Stare You In The Face."

Sam Adams has done his work well. An estimated five thousand people appear, overflowing into the streets around Faneuil Hall. Before the morning is over, they shout their approval of a resolution demanding that the tea be sent back to England.

There is a legal loophole, however. A rule exists that customs officers can seize a cargo if duty payments are not made within twenty days. So, if the *Dartmouth*'s cargo isn't landed by December 17th, that is, physically placed on the docks and consigned to the importers, British customs officials in Boston can claim it, auction it off, and still assess the Townshend duty. Protest would be useless.

The *Dartmouth*, now tied up at Griffin's Wharf, comes under round-the-clock patriot guard. Soon, she is joined by the *Eleanor*, also carrying East India tea. By the 15th, the brig *Beaver* has arrived, with more tea aboard.

Throughout the past two weeks, there have been bitter exchanges between the patriots and the loyalist importers, who stand to make a fine profit. A desperate Governor Hutchinson is in the middle. Yet not an ounce of tea has come ashore from the steadily patrolled docks.

Rain pelts Boston all day on December 16th, the day before customs can legally seize the cargoes, but the weather doesn't deter the patriots from a last minute meeting at Old South Hall. They enter the hall damp but determined, rain beading on their heavy coats and tricornered hats, their faces red from the cold.

In late afternoon, Sam Adams finally and sadly admits "that nothing can be done to save the country." But his tongue is wagging in his cheek. It is a facetious remark, probably spoken for the benefit of any loyalists who may be present. Something *will* be done. It has already been expertly planned, principally by Adams and Hancock.

There are responding shouts from the audience in Old South Hall. Among the shouts are, "Boston harbor a teapot tonight."

Not long after the meeting breaks up, a few patriots dressed as Mohawk Indians, others more simply disguised by smears of burnt cork on their faces, move down Hutchinson Street and then to Griffin's Wharf. So begins the "tea party," a bit after six, the moon coming out to help illuminate the shadowy men smashing tea chests with axes. All three vessels are boarded.

By nine o'clock, more than ninety thousand pounds of tea are floating in Boston harbor. It coats the hulls of the vessels at waterline and piles in layers inches deep over the frigid surface, finally drifting away on the tide.

"This is the Most Magnificent Movement of all," glowed John Adams in his diary the next day. "There is a Dignity, a Majesty, a Sublimity in this last Effort of the Patriots that I greatly admire. This Destruction of Tea is so bold, so daring, so firm, so intrepid, inflexible . . . that I cannot but consider it an Epoch in History . . ."

This is typical John Adams, but official London, on learning of the tea party, sees little majesty or dignity in it. Parliament is shocked and Townshend is in a towering rage.

However, most of the people in the colonies applaud Boston's action as postriders carry the news on their regular routes. Because of the protests, tea ships cannot unload in New York or Philadelphia. Only a small amount of the six hundred thousand pounds ever reaches cups in America.

For months afterward, there are incidents up and down the Atlantic seaboard. A shipment consigned to Prentis & Company, on Duke of Gloucester Street, is dumped into the York River by patriots. Aside from this minor flurry, there are no overt acts of protest in Virginia and the uneasy quiet of five years is more or less maintained.

In fact, Williamsburg is exceedingly gracious when Lady Dunmore finally arrives with her brood of three daughters and three sons. The welcome is warm and sincere as Mayor Dixon orders another Grand Illumination. After too long a time, the laughter of children will be heard in the Governor's Palace, and they will be seen playing in the hedged gardens behind it. This pleases the people and Lady Dunmore will undoubtedly add to the social graces of the Tidewater.

In London this spring of 1774, Parliament, understandably, is outraged by the incidents concerning the ships, particularly the humiliating tea party. To curb the effrontery of the upstart colonists, Parliament has passed the Boston Port Bill, five acts to become known as the Intolerable Acts. No longer will England put up with lawlessness in the American colonies. Effective June 1st, the port of Boston will be closed until such time as the colony pays for the destroyed tea. Boston will be cut off from the sea and all vital commerce. Boston makes its living from the sea, so the port bill is a drastic step.

Furthermore, Massachusetts loses its right of self-government for an undetermined period. A third measure makes it possible to send anyone accused of murder in connection with law enforcement to England for trial. Four regiments of Redcoats will now enforce the law throughout the colony; General Gage, commander of British troops in America, will become the governor. It will be martial law at the end of Queen Bess muskets.

In the view of many colonists, the London action cannot and will not be tolerated. With the Boston patriots' studied resistance at Griffin's Wharf, and with Parliament's firm plan for punishment scheduled to begin within weeks, the course toward revolution is finally set.

On May 24th, the Virginia burgesses unite behind a resolution prepared by Patrick Henry, Thomas Jefferson, and those always-ready Lees, Richard H. and Francis L. Even the staunch conservative Robert Carter Nicholas, every vein in his body loyal to the Crown, introduces it in a show of solidarity: "This House, being deeply impressed with the Apprehension of the great Dangers, to be derived to British America, from the hostile Invasion of the City of Boston, in our Sister Colony of Massachusetts Bay, where Commerce and Harbor are, on the first day of June, next, to be stopped by an Armed Force, deem it highly necessary that the said first day of June be set apart, by members of this House, as a day of Fasting, Humiliation and Prayer. . . ."

Receiving a copy of the resolution, Lord Dunmore immediately dissolves the Assembly. He cannot let the burgesses' brazen insolence toward the Crown go unnoticed.

As in 1769, they politely obey his bidding and then reassemble the next day in the less formal atmosphere of the Apollo Room at the Raleigh Tavern. Quickly calling for another boycott of British goods, they then take a much more important stride along the road to independence by proposing that a general congress of all the colonies meet in Philadelphia in September. It will be known as the First Continental Congress.

The proposal is perhaps the most significant step the Virginia burgesses have ever taken. If the other colonies agree to meet in such a congress, it may mean the beginning of a colonial political organization that will be independent of England. The fact that they name it the First Continental Congress indicates they hope to hold a second, a third, and perhaps even more meetings. Copies of the resolution go out to all the other colonies through the Committee on Correspondence.

While the furor over the Stamp Act rallied the colonies, the Intolerable Acts are forging them into even greater unity. While the Stamp Act Congress was called to deal with one issue, the new congress will deal with all issues of the conflict between England and the colonies.

During this smoldering, deliberate period, patriot George Mason ventures down from his plantation at Gunston Hall on business and spends an evening with Patrick Henry. Discussing the Boston tea party and other things, they find they have much in common, particularly where England is concerned.

Owner of a seven thousand acre plantation on Pohick Creek, along the banks of the Potomac, next to Washington's Mount Vernon, Mason has attempted to stay out of public office but is still a political leader of great stature. Though not a lawyer, the burly dark-haired man commands great attention as a speaker and writer and as a man of wisdom and perception.

The day after their meeting, Mason writes of Patrick Henry, ". . . his eloquence is the smallest part of his merit. He is, in my opinion, the first man on the continent." Mason's opinion is by no means universally shared. Henry is still detested and feared by many conservatives. He seems too belligerent, his tongue too capable of arousing passions.

June 1st is the day set aside for "fasting and prayer." About ten o'clock in the morning, with the sergeant at arms carrying the silver mace, the symbol of authority, Speaker Peyton Randolph, a mountain of dignity in his robes of office, leads the burgesses from the Capitol along Duke of Gloucester Street to Bruton Church while shopkeepers and townspeople watch.

In a double line, tricornered hats bobbing, they move up the street, faces solemn. It is a silent, impressive protest against the Intolerable Acts, and soon the Reverend Price preaches a sermon in tribute to the *Friends, Brethren, and Countrymen* of Boston, beleaguered by martial law at this hour.

Lord Dunmore is helpless to do anything about this dissident congregation. Cannot men swear off food for a day? Cannot men gather in a house of worship to pray?

In August, the First Virginia Convention of delegates convenes to discuss colony matters and elect representatives to the upcoming First Continental Congress in Philadelphia. Each colony had welcomed Virginia's proposal. The meeting at the Capitol this morning is unique. This is not an assembly authorized by the Crown but a voluntary gathering of Virginia's political leaders for the purpose of opposing England on certain issues. In the other colonies, men were similarly meeting to elect delegates to the Philadelphia congress.

Though Thomas Jefferson is not present because of illness, he has forwarded his thoughts from his Monticello estate to Patrick Henry and Peyton Randolph. Contained in a paper entitled "A Summary View of the Rights of British America," they are judged too inflammatory to present to the congress in Philadelphia, but Randolph reads them to a stellar group of patriots in his Market Square home.

Then they are set into type by Clementina Rind, Williamsburg's only woman printer, and are soon sold in town. Later, they also appear in the Philadelphia press, so that delegates to the Continental Congress can study them anyway, radical views or not.

Jefferson, it is revealed, believes in dealing firmly with England.

Traveling north to Philadelphia in late August, Edmund Pendleton and Henry stop first at Gunston Hall to collect George Mason. Then the three ride on to Mount Vernon where they spend the night of August 30th with the Washingtons, dining and talking. The following day, Colonel

Mason returns home, while the others begin the long journey to Quaker town, riding up through Maryland and Delaware.

Martha Washington bids them good-bye, reportedly saying to Henry and Pendleton, "I hope you will stand firm. I know George will."

Along with Randolph, Richard Bland, Benjamin Harrison, and Richard Henry Lee, they are Virginia's delegates to the First Continental Congress. They go with some pride since their proposal had set in motion the plans for the congress.

For the sake of Lord Dunmore's appetite and nerves, it is just as well that he hasn't been in Williamsburg the past few weeks, while the delegates were being elected and Jefferson's paper was being circulated. Dunmore has traveled to the Ohio River, with the Virginia militia, to negotiate with the Shawnee Indians. They have been harassing settlers of late.

# 9 Liberty or Death

King George's message to Parliament on the opening day of the November session in London is finally printed in the *Virginia Gazettes* in early February, 1775.

There are two newspapers of that name, and eventually a third one will exist, each published by different editors. It is easy to become confused

about which *Gazette* printed what. Was the story
in Purdie's *Gazette*? Or was it in Pinkney's or
Dixon-Hunter's *Gazette*? The newspapers vary politically. They are, of course, an important means
of communication for the people of Williamsburg.

But George III's speech does not require much
interpretation. Angry with Massachusetts' "spirit
of resistance and disobedience to the law," the
monarch stated, "I have taken measures and given
such orders . . . for carrying into execution the
laws which were passed in the last session of the
late Parliament . . ." He is referring, of course, to
the Intolerable Acts.

At about the same time, Prime Minister Lord
North makes an even tougher speech in the House
of Commons, also reported in the *Gazettes*. North
proposes to send four more regiments of Redcoats
to General Gage to put down any other displays of
rebellion in the colonies. If the colonies refuse to
trade with Great Britain, he threatens to impose a
sea blockade. No ships, of any flag, will be able to
load or unload cargoes. If carried out, the blockade
could economically strangle the colonies.

On these two warning notes, March has arrived.
The Second Virginia Convention is meeting in
Richmond's St. John's Church, on a wooded hill
above Shockoe Creek. The site has been chosen for

its distance from the suspicious eyes and sensitive ears of Lord Dunmore, four months returned from the Shawnee Indian unrest on the Ohio River. This convention of the colony's political leaders will discuss colonial matters and, more importantly, elect delegates to the Second Continental Congress, scheduled to meet in Philadelphia in May.

Almost all of the burgesses are present, assembled at the white wooden church enclosed by the usual brick wall. The horses and carriages of Patrick Henry, George Washington, Thomas Jefferson, Edmund Pendleton, Peyton Randolph, the Lees, and others are lined at the hitching rails or beneath newly budded branches beyond the wall.

The First Virginia Convention of August past, at the Capitol, one that would have made Dunmore's blood percolate had he been in Williamsburg, was occupied with protests against the Boston Port Bill, the boycott of British goods, and the election of delegates to the first congress in Philadelphia.

In Richmond now, the delegates expect to explore beyond those issues. Oddly enough, in spite of the King's stern remarks and Lord North's ominous threats, the conservatives, especially, still have great hope for a reconciliation with England.

In fact, with the exception of Patrick Henry and a very few others, no citizen in any of the colonies has given serious thought to independence. Up to now, even Henry has not publicly uttered his views on the possibility of independence. For the vast majority of people, it was a staggering move to contemplate.

And Lord North had recently spoken in softer tones. Also, popular sentiment in England was reported to be for the colonists and not the Crown. Word from London was that most Britishers thought Parliament and the King had been too harsh.

The first two days at St. John's Church are rather routine with a review of the proceedings at the First Continental Congress. Although nothing of great importance was accomplished in Philadelphia, the congress had brought the colonial leaders together. They had talked in committee and wined and dined together at Daniel Smyth's fine City Tavern.

Henry had met Sam Adams, at last, and John Adams, the astute New Englander destined to become the second president of a new nation. Personal bonds had been formed between like-minded men. Henry, for one, had told the Philadelphia delegates, "The distinction between Virginians, Pennsylvanians, New Yorkers, and New Englanders are no more. I am not a Virginian, but an American." The old feeling of each colony "going it alone" was almost gone.

On this balmy morning of March 23rd, with birds chittering in the trees and spectators milling about outside the church, some listening through open windows, Henry wins Peyton Randolph's approval to submit a resolution.

The clerk drones it out, beginning with the words, "Resolved, That a well regulated militia, composed of Gentlemen and Yeomen, is the natural strength, and only security of a free government . . ."

On and on it went until the clerk read, "Resolved, therefore, That this colony be immediately put into a posture of defence . . ." The shocking Patrick Henry has shocked again.

Gasps are heard and frowns appear on some faces. "A posture of defence" means a formal army. Henry is proposing that two regiments be established in Virginia. An army is good for only one thing—to fight!

The clerk finishes and the chair again recognizes Mr. Henry, who rises, standing in a pew on the left-hand side of the church, facing the altar. As usual, his voice is quiet and calm as he begins.

"There is no longer room for hope. If we wish to be free—if we mean to preserve inviolate those inestimable privileges for which we have been so long contending . . . we must fight. . . ."

There is a stir all over St. John's.

Different versions of the speech in support of his resolution get back to Williamsburg, some more legendary than truthful, but all versions agree that the delegates sat transfixed, staring in awe at the lanky, wiry, dark-suited, dark-faced burgess.

"Gentlemen may cry peace, peace—but there is no peace. The next gale that sweeps from the north will bring to our ears the clash of resounding arms. Our brethren are already in the field . . ."

He is referring to the colonists of Massachusetts Bay who are living under the guns of General Gage.

"Why stand we here idle? What is it that gentlemen wish? What would they have?"

All the oratorical timing, the gestures, the dramatic pauses—everything learned over the years in the courtrooms and in the House of Burgesses—are brought to full play in the hushed church.

"Is life so dear or peace so sweet, as to be purchased at the price of chains and slavery?"

Spectator John Roane said that Henry was now

"standing in the attitude of a condemned galley slave, loaded with fetters, awaiting his doom. His wrists were crossed; manacles almost visible . . ."

"Forbid it, Almighty God," Henry intones.

Roane reported that he "raised his eyes and chained hands toward heaven."

Then Henry turns toward the conservatives to finish. "I know not what course others take, but as for me, give me liberty, or give me death."

There is silence in St. John's as Mr. Henry resumes his seat. For a moment, the only sound is birdsong, penetrating from the trees outside. The men leaning through the windows, crammed head and shoulder, seem impaled. (One makes a request to be buried beneath the window through which he leaned. In time, it is granted.)

Richard Henry Lee stands up to be recognized and breaks the spell. He speaks in behalf of the resolution, offering the seconding motion. Jefferson, never skilled at oratory, and Thomas Nelson, Jr., follow to lend support.

By now, Henry's old opponents, the conservatives, have recovered. One by one, they argue against the resolve, still hoping to maintain peace with England by negotiation. Often, it seems these men are more against Henry personally than against the ideas he expresses. Emotionally, they often appear to agree with him. Yet they also seem afraid that he will lead them into war with his reckless tongue.

There is nothing particularly new in what Henry has proposed. A Virginia militia already exists. There has been such a home defense force for years, authorized and controlled by the colonial assembly. Yet, what Henry is suggesting sounds very much like an "army," one that might be used for more than defense against Indian attack or slave uprising. And lingering in the air are his words, "If we wish to be free . . . we must fight. . . ."

Aided by the stunning oratory, the resolution passes 65 to 60, indicating again the narrow margin between the progressives and the conservatives. Henry is selected to head the committee that will organize, equip, and train two regiments. The step is certain to cause concern, if not alarm, in the Governor's Palace and in London.

Now that the convention has gone this far, Robert Carter Nicholas, burning at the thought of Henry's resolution, moves to organize ten thousand troops instead of the one thousand the Hanover legislator proposed. The measure goes down to defeat. Since Nicholas had voted against the Henry resolve, his amendment appears to be a statement of ridicule.

As the meeting adjourns, what optimism the conservatives held for mending relations with England has once again been shattered, and by the same man. The frustration and alarm of Pendleton and the other moderates grow.

On Saturday, the convention elects representatives to the Second Continental Congress, slated to convene in the Quaker City on May 10th. The same faces will return and neither Lord Dunmore nor the King will be happy about it. In fact, George III issues a proclamation against the "unjustifiable proceedings" in Philadelphia.

The colonists ignore it.

# 10 The Magazine Is Raided

Under a moon bright and innocent, five days past full, Williamsburg sleeps this night of April 20–21, 1775. A few lusty snores can be heard in the inns and boardinghouses but there is little disturbance elsewhere.

The shadows around the Capitol are scarcely ominous, and Duke of Gloucester Street, scented with the awakening of yet another spring, is deserted. Market Square is ghostly but friendly in the ivory light; the Powder Magazine, opposite the courthouse, is a dark blob.

Why shouldn't the townspeople sleep peacefully? In spite of Patrick Henry's dramatic oratory at St. John's and his proposal to organize two regiments; in spite of the fact that Lord Dunmore has placed an armed schooner, the *Magdalen*, off Burwell's Ferry in the placid James River just four miles south of town, war with England seems no closer than it did a year ago.

But no one in the entire colony of Virginia, no matter how good his sources of information, is aware that in Massachusetts Paul Revere has already made his midnight ride. *The first shots of the American revolution have been fired.* After a British attack, a group of patriots, the Minute Men, fought and died on Lexington Common and at Concord Bridge. Smoke and the smell of battle are still in the air in the northern colony.

Patrick Henry had been prophetic when he said only a month before, "The next gale that sweeps from the north will bring to our ears the clash of resounding arms."

Tensions have been high since General Gage's occupation of Massachusetts began. That, and British attempts to destroy military supplies being gathered by the partiots, made a clash inevitable.

In Williamsburg, it is now between 3 and 4 A.M., with the sun scheduled to splash its yellow light across the plantations at five thirty. Suddenly, there is movement on the grounds of the Governor's Palace. A small wagon rolls along, and with it walk fifteen British Marines off the *Magdalen*, under the command of Lieutenant Henry Collins.

Last week, Easter week, Lord Dunmore had demanded the keys to the Powder Magazine from Keeper John Miller. Twenty-one and a half barrels of dry, precious powder are stored there, along with muskets. Dunmore ordered Miller to remove the firing pieces from the muskets.

The powder and arms are for the defense of the colony against an Indian attack or a slave uprising. In the people's opinion, the powder belongs to them, not to the Crown. Miller quickly reported the incident to the town, and volunteer guards took up posts outside the brick building. But after a few days and nights, when no attempt was made to spirit the powder away, the guards relaxed. In fact, this morning they are at home asleep, like everyone else.

The wagon rolls on through the predawn darkness, making little noise. It moves out onto Duke of Gloucester Street, then cuts across to the unguarded magazine. A single locked gate in the high brick wall is the only means of entrance.

Collins has it opened with the "borrowed" key. The transfer of fifteen and a half barrels of powder to his lordship's wagon doesn't take long. The wagon begins to move again.

Incredibly, the plot is Dunmore's own, hatched without urging from England or the British military. Aside from Collins and his raiders, plus the sailors on the *Magdalen*, no British armed forces are stationed near Williamsburg, anyway. Dunmore is attempting the same action that General Gage has already taken in Massachusetts. It is a clear move to deprive the Virginia colonists of the means to take up arms.

The wagon rolls on. Somewhere between Market Square and Burwell's Ferry an early riser discovers the nocturnal procession and sounds the alarm.

Williamsburg awakens to shouts and the roll of drums. Within a short time, citizens are thronging the steps of James City Courthouse and spreading out onto the green. Men of the Independent Company of militia, organized the year before mainly

for Dunmore's "war" against the Shawnees, arrive with muskets.

With only a few slaves and staff members on hand, and only a small arsenal on the first floor, Dunmore is almost defenseless in the palace. By this time, Lieutenant Collins is well away from Williamsburg; perhaps already sailing for Norfolk to relay the purloined powder to HMS *Fowey*, a larger ship.

Dunmore later wrote to Lord Dartmouth, the British secretary of state: "All the people assembled and during their consultations continuous threats were brought to my House, that it was their Resolution to seize upon me, or massacre me, and every person found giving me assistance, if I refused to deliver the Powder immediately to their custody."

Mayor Dixon, some of the aldermen, and several members of the Council, as well as other men with cooler heads such as Peyton Randolph, prevail against the shouting crowd. They suggest to the mob that a petition be sent to Dunmore. Hurriedly written, it is meekly worded and gives Dunmore a "face-saving" excuse to return the barrels. It stresses the need for the powder as protection for the colony.

Then Dixon and the Independent Company,

followed by the crowd, advance up the Palace Green. The armed company and the tense townspeople come to a halt halfway up the wide lawn, opposite George Wythe's house, while Dixon and the Council members continue on. Presumably, Dunmore is watching from an upper window.

It might have looked like a scene from a comic opera, but gunpowder had long been an important means of survival for the colonists. Confiscation by anyone, governor or king, would always bring armed men on the run.

Finally, Dixon confronts his lordship with the mildly worded petition. Later Dunmore will describe it as ". . . if not a treasonable proceeding, at least nothing less than one of the highest insults that could be offered to the Authority of His Majesty's Government."

Though in the past he hasn't appeared to frighten easily, the Scots nobleman is alarmed this time and assures Dixon that the powder will be returned should a slave uprising occur. But he doesn't offer to summon it back. Rather, he threatens to defend the palace by arming the slaves with guns from his small arsenal.

Dixon now has the unpleasant task of informing the waiting crowd. Dunmore's refusal to return the powder is met with anger, but various men, primarily Peyton Randolph and Robert Carter Nicholas, persuade the townspeople to disband, to go back to their homes and jobs. Gradually, they disperse but feeling still runs high.

The next day, Dr. William Pasteur, medicine bag in hand, leaves his apothecary shop on Duke of Gloucester Street to go to the palace a few blocks away. A patient needs treatment. While there, Dr. Pasteur is himself treated to some unsolicited lecturing about the colony by Lord Dunmore, who is in a terrible pique.

Scurrying away, the physician reports that the governor has sworn ". . . by the Living God that if a grain of powder is burnt at Captain Foy or Captain Collins or if any Injury or Insult is offered to himself, that he would declare Freedom to the slaves and reduce the city of Williamsburg to ashes."

His is the indignation of a caught thief.

Word of the powder seizure spreads quickly and on April 25th, Fredericksburg's Independent Company notifies its leader, Colonel George Washington, that, with his approval, it will be ready to start for the capital to "appear in support of the honor of Virginia." Similar messages also arrive from the Independent Companies of Prince William and Albemarle counties.

Four days later, one hundred and two men, representing a total body of almost seven hundred colonial volunteers, meet in Fredericksburg to discuss a march to the James River, but after a letter from Peyton Randolph is read, they disperse quietly. Randolph assures them that the powder incident has been satisfactorily resolved.

Nonetheless, they publicly state: "We do now pledge ourselves to each other to be in readiness, at a moment's notice, to reassemble, and by forces of arms defend the law, the liberty and rights of this or any sister colony, from unjust and wicked invasion."

On this same day, the people of Williamsburg finally learn the grim news from Lexington Common and Concord Bridge. Alexander Purdie's *Gazette* comments, "The Sword is now drawn, and God knows when it will be sheathed." John Pinkney's *Gazette* says, "The Blow is now struck, a great deal of Blood spilt. . . ."

# 11 Meet Me in Arms at New Castle

Patrick Henry has moved from Louisa County and has been watching events from his new Scotchtown estate in Hanover County. He is enraged on learning that the Fredericksburg men have called off their mission to bring Lord Dunmore to heel by musket force. Henry is for striking a blow—"at once, before an overwhelming force should enter the colony," he tells Colonel Richard Morris.

He then passes word to the officers and men of the Independent Company of Hanover, a group he formed months before at Smith's Tavern, near Richmond, to meet him "in arms at New Castle, on the Second of May, on business of the highest importance to American liberty."

It is later reported that he maintains the people should be made to "see and feel their strength by being brought out together; that the revolution should be set in actual motion in the colony now . . ."

It is precisely this type of belligerent reaction that causes both anger and anxiety in such men as Edmund Pendleton and Peyton Randolph. The latter's peace-making efforts can be quickly upset by some choice and sizzling Hanover oratory.

The Governor's Palace is edgy, too. The threats of the townspeople on April 21st obviously linger in Dunmore's mind. Observers see the heavily laden royal coach, with Lady Dunmore and the children as passengers, trail out of town on the last day of April. Their destination is the HMS *Fowey*, now anchored on more or less permanent "Virginia station" off Yorktown, the nearby hamlet on the York River.

By twilight, on May 3rd, exercising his rank of "captain" in the Independents for the first time, Patrick Henry arrives with his insurgent band, variously estimated at sixty, one hundred and fifty, and five hundred, at Doncastle's Ordinary, a tavern about sixteen miles from Williamsburg. News of his march from Hanover has reached nearby counties and more men are making plans to join him. Coming in the wake of the news from Massachusetts, the Henry march provokes great excitement in those ready to fight the British, fear and helplessness in the moderates.

At the palace, Dunmore is informed of the presence of Henry's little army, and at midnight the governor sends a message to Captain James Montagu, on the *Fowey*, requesting military aid. He flatly claims he is about to be attacked. From all reports, Henry *is* actually hoping for a confrontation.

Meanwhile, plantation owner Carter Braxton, a new member of the House of Burgesses, and others have ridden to Doncastle's to meet with Henry in an effort to stop the march. Worried that Dunmore might carry out his threat to burn Williamsburg, they are also concerned that the *Fowey*'s cannon might be turned on defenseless Yorktown. Finally, Henry agrees to remain at Doncastle's while Braxton and his associates negotiate with Dunmore for the return of the powder.

On the *Fowey*, already an uneasy home for Lady Dunmore and the children, marines and sailors assemble for the short trek to Williamsburg. Under Captain Stretch, there are forty-three men, quite enough to make it lively for Henry should he open fire. In a few hours, they take up posts in the palace guardroom on the first floor.

By now, Braxton has returned to Williamsburg and with Thomas Nelson, Sr., president of the Council, he begins a parley with Richard Corbin, the receiver general, the colony's chief finance executive.

In the early morning, they ride again for Doncastle's, and by day's end, Patrick Henry has written: "Received from the Honourable Richard Corbin, Esq., His Majesty's receiver-general, £330, as compensation for the gunpowder lately taken out of the Public magazine by the governor's orders. . . ."

Henry dismisses his volunteers and returns to his Scotchtown estate, having somewhat satisfied Virginia's honor. But Dunmore soon issues a proclamation against the Hanover burgess accusing him of treason. Later, Dunmore writes an explanation to Lord Dartmouth: "A party headed by a certain Patrick Henry, one of the Delegates of this Colony, a Man of desperate Circumstances, and one who has been very active in encouraging Disobedience and exciting a Spirit of Revolt among the People for many Years past, advanced to within a few Miles of this Place, and there encamped with all the Appearances of actual War."

Mr. Henry and others would have to agree with that account.

# 12 Dunmore Flees

By mid-May, 1775, it often seems that Williamsburg is being used to gather troops for another of those bloody wars against the French and Indians. The sound of drum and fife can be heard; orders to "attack" and "retreat" are thudded out as the militia occasionally drills. Fourteen is the perfect age for drummer boys and they are being recruited.

While they do not discuss it at great length, the Virginians are preparing for the possibility of British attack.

Around town can be seen rough-looking men clad in homespun shirts that fall almost to their knees. Sometimes a scalping knife or a tomahawk hangs from their belts. Though not soldiers, these weather-beaten "Shirtmen," with skin as coarse as the neck of an old plucked turkey, are excellent shots, especially good at sighting down the barrels of squirrel rifles.

There is anticipation in the air. People eagerly buy each new edition of the *Gazettes*, looking for accounts of resistance in other colonies. They scan the news from Massachusetts Bay, where the Redcoats are still in command.

Patrick Henry has already ridden off to join Virginia's other political leaders in Philadelphia for the meeting of the Second Continental Congress, and the *Gazettes* soon report that the "spirit of defiance is very evident." Some of the New England delegates have traveled part of the way south with a militia escort. Word had filtered out that they might be arrested by the British en route to Philadelphia.

Yet, Williamsburg is rather placid during this period of a struggle of words—at least, on the surface. Lord Dunmore's family has returned from the decks of the *Fowey*. They are home again in the palace and their presence helps to ease the tension. The emergency over, Captain Stretch and the Royal Marines have departed the grounds for Yorktown.

Soon, Peyton Randolph arrives from Philadelphia to resume his chair as speaker of the House of Burgesses, which is about to convene. In what is nearly a "hero's welcome," he is met far on the outskirts of town by a group of volunteer cavalrymen; closer in, a company of volunteer infantrymen join the escort.

As Randolph rides onto Duke of Gloucester Street, with troops on either side of him, the bell of Bruton Church tolls out to pay homage, and that night Williamsburg honors him with a candle display. Beyond his contributions as president of the Second Continental Congress, the portly speaker has defied the Crown, of course, merely by attending the colonial meeting. He is a visible symbol of resistance and the town is filled with pride. Randolph will return to the Quaker City when the Assembly adjourns.

The proceedings in Philadelphia are in Dunmore's opinion illegal. Whatever his feelings, however, his opening-day speech to the General

Assembly is not antagonistic. He reviews Lord
North's February speech in which the Britisher
made a sincere attempt to reconcile the colonies
with the mother country. The Scots governor
holds out an official hand of peace and friendship,
too, though largely on England's terms. Lord Dunmore exclaims, "The King has no object nearer his
heart than the peace and prosperity of his subjects
in every part of the dominion."

Somehow, in view of the Boston Port Bill and
the bloodshed at Lexington Common and Concord
Bridge, the words sound log hollow to those assembled in the hall.

The next day, Friday, the burgesses communicate to the palace that Dunmore's speech is under
study and that the governor will receive a reply to
it in time. Among others, Thomas Jefferson, who
is scheduled to depart in a few days for Philadelphia as Randolph's alternate to the congress, is appointed to draft a letter of response.

Dunmore, it is later learned, has little hope that
the reply will be favorable. However, he still in-
vites some of the burgesses to dinner on this Friday as a further show of friendship and goodwill.
To the man, they decline.

Saturday night, a gunshot is heard from the vi-
cinity of the Powder Magazine. Those who live

nearby hop out of bed. Nightcapped heads push through open windows. Lanterns in the gloom reveal that three local boys have been wounded by a musket trap rigged for prowlers. One is Mayor Dixon's son.

The boys had been up to no good, of course; they had been attempting to break into the magazine. But that fact is quickly lost in the outcry. Another trap is discovered, and the blame is placed on the governor. Likely, Captain Stretch and his marines had rigged the treacherous trap before returning to Yorktown. The townspeople find it difficult to believe that Dunmore didn't know about the cocked muskets.

On Monday, the new incident is the main topic of conversation in Williamsburg. The thought of local youth being blown apart by string-triggered guns provides the opportunity for another protest. By noon, however, Dunmore is himself in position to make some sharp remarks about lawlessness. A crowd of citizens has descended on the magazine, broken into it, and carried off about four hundred guns.

For forty-eight hours, the burgesses and Dunmore are at a standoff; they exchange cool notes. However, no one is prepared for the governor's next move. Around 2 A.M., Thursday, while the town slumbers, the governor, his Lady, and the children, along with Captain Foy and a few servants, slip away from the palace and head for Yorktown in the royal coach. They take sanctuary aboard the *Fowey*.

His good-bye message is read to the astonished Assembly in the morning:

"Mr. Speaker and Gentlemen of the House of Burgesses—Being now fully persuaded that my Person, and those of my Family likewise, are in constant danger of falling sacrifices to the blind and unmeasurable fury which has so unaccountably seized upon the minds and understanding of great numbers of People, and apprehending that at length some of them may work themselves up to that pitch of daringness and atrociousness as to fall upon me . . . I have thought it Prudent to remove myself. . . ."

Concluding his message with instructions for the Assembly to continue its business and report to him from time to time, he signed it, curtly, "Dunmore."

Although the governor was abidingly disliked by almost everyone, few people, if any, meant him physical harm. Lady Dunmore, being very popular, was certainly in no danger. The children would never have been harmed. The townspeople, as well as the burgesses, are puzzled.

It is then discovered, however, that on the previous evening his lordship had walked to loyalist Attorney General John Randolph's house, a quarter mile from the palace. Perhaps someone had met him in the shadows, threatening him bodily. More likely, though, Dunmore saw nothing but trouble ahead and based his decision to flee on the cloudy future.

For the next two weeks, messages flow back and forth between the Capitol and the quarterdeck of the *Fowey*. There are charges and countercharges.

Judging from reports in the weekly *Gazettes*, it has been strangely quiet in Carpenter's Hall in Philadelphia. In part, the silence is explained by the fact that there is much to do in the City of Brotherly Love: Attempts are being made to organize some kind of national government, create an army, select a leader for it, raise funds to supply the troops, and, not the least, make another sincere appeal to the Crown to understand the position of the colonies.

Independence may or may not be inevitable. Meanwhile, plans must be made. From everywhere come other signs of the collapse of British rule such as that evidenced in Williamsburg by Dunmore's abrupt departure. The colonists must prepare for the worst—war and independence.

On June 15th a major accomplishment occurs in Carpenter's Hall. Colonel George Washington, the man who gave up "soldiering" because he didn't like it, is unanimously elected by congress as commander-in-chief of the revolutionary armies, a post John Hancock had wanted. Edmund Pendleton had opposed Washington at first, perhaps because he had been close to the Henry-Jefferson-Lee group of militants, but then supported him.

Two days later, fighting flares again in Massachusetts. Patriot forces entrenched on Bunker Hill, opposite Boston, are driven back, but only after heavy losses to the Redcoats. The patriots serve notice that they will be tough opponents. They do not retreat until their gunpowder is exhausted.

The following day Washington, Philip Schuyler, and that brawling, profane British renegade Charles Lee, all now new generals, leave Ben Franklin's town for Massachusetts. Washington will take over command of the New England militiamen at Cambridge and lay siege to the city of Boston. There seems to be optimism along his

route. Bands play and a cavalry parade is staged in his honor as he rides out.

Before the *Gazettes* can print the exciting news that a Virginian has been chosen as commander-in-chief of the armies, it is time to dismiss a slightly confused General Assembly, a step heretofore taken only with the permission of the governor. Abiding by past rules, the burgesses send a request for adjournment to Yorktown. Still petulant, Dunmore won't make the decision. Neither will he return to Williamsburg to sign some awaiting bills. Bring them down, he orders.

So, on Saturday, June 24, 1775, the Assembly gathers to adopt its final resolution for the session. Bowing to long tradition, the body declares its continuing "affection for, and allegiance to, the King." That done, the burgesses promptly disband without authority.

For all intents and purposes, there is no longer any British control at the seat of government in Virginia. Although the members of the upper house of the Assembly are royal appointees, they have no authority to act in an executive capacity. Attorney General John Randolph, still very much loyal to the Crown and thinking about sailing for England, cannot assume authority. Dunmore, though absent, is still governor. It all adds up to a feeling of being adrift, and this same night, as the legislators head for their home counties, the palace arsenal is robbed. The danger of lawlessness hangs over the colony.

That Dunmore probably will not return without an army of Redcoats becomes apparent a few days later when Lady Dunmore and the children sail for England. His lordship goes as far as Norfolk with them and then returns to Yorktown. In a short time, he sails again, this time to set up headquarters in Norfolk, intent upon punishing the disloyal colonists.

# 13 "Colonel" Henry Now

Edmund Pendleton, still recognizing Lord Dunmore as the legal ruling authority in Virginia, apparently still hopeful of closing the ever-widening breach with England, is selected to head the Committee of Safety by the Third Virginia Convention of delegates, meeting in Richmond in August, 1775. This committee will take the place, temporarily, of a governor and Council. It will operate as an executive branch. Pendleton, in effect, becomes leader of Virginia's government.

The Committee of Safety is given extraordinary powers, including control of troops in the field, the authority to raise arms, the right to enter into negotiations with other colonies for military support, and even the power to seize and imprison Tories, or loyalists as Crown sympathizers were known, if they endangered the colony. Quickly, military service for all able-bodied men, excepting the British-born, is made mandatory.

No doubt that new military officer, *Colonel* Patrick Henry, was rather discouraged to see his old political foe, Pendleton, in charge of the Committee of Safety. From Colonel Henry's viewpoint, the group will automatically move in cautious ways.

Henry's commission as colonel is approved by the convention delegates August 23rd, and three weeks later, as Virginia's first military commander-in-chief, he arrives in Williamsburg to take up his duties. He will command the troops authorized by the Second Virginia Convention in answer to his "Give me liberty, or give me death" speech. Of late, Henry has wanted a military career to match his dazzling political career. Now, he has prospects of it. A man such as Henry could easily see himself triumphing over the Redcoats. He did not lack in confidence.

He inspects the grounds around the town and then selects an area behind the college for encampment of his troops. It is a fact that he has had no military experience aside from the bloodless march to Doncastle's. He's never even skirmished with Indians. But few men in any of the colonies have been trained to lead troops. Henry's appointment is purely political, courtesy of his many delegate friends. They had placed his name before the convention and he had won the commander's job over more experienced candidates.

In a few weeks, nine companies of militia are in Williamsburg. The ruddy men from Culpeper County wear green hunting shirts with "Liberty or Death" emblazoned on their backs, a slogan calculated to please Colonel Henry. At this point, the troops are Virginia's "army" for defense against the British.

But it is a poor army that is gathering in Williamsburg. There is little gunpowder, not enough tents for the troops. Each man is required to bring his own blanket and clothing. Many carry their own guns. Yet their presence in town is comforting. By chill night, their campfires dot the darkness behind the College of William and Mary.

As the winter of 1775–1776 approaches, Lord Dunmore is still firmly entrenched in the Norfolk area. Living aboard the man-of-war *Royal William*, anchored in a fork of the brown, meandering Elizabeth River at a place called Gosport, below Portsmouth Village and across from Norfolk, he is sending out raiding parties to plunder the plantations and enlist slaves. His greatest need is food for the expanding naval force and a tiny but growing army. Plainly, Dunmore plans to fight and regain control of Virginia. He has requested troops from England.

While waiting for them to arrive, the governor is acting more like a warlord than a political executive. He now has a considerable fleet: four men-of-war, four schooners, three sloops, and three tenders. They are adequate to harass and blockade most rebel commercial shipping around Hampton Roads. It is also reported that Dunmore has seized the printing press of a rebellious Norfolk editor who had stuck verbal pins in his Scotch hide, and that he has personally engaged in battle with patriot groups. More of a direct threat, though, is his arming of the slaves. He plans to form an "Ethiopian Corps."

So it is only a matter of time before the Committee of Safety will have to deal with the intracta-

ble Lord Dunmore. The sooner the better, many
people in Williamsburg think. He cannot be per-
mitted to raid the Norfolk area indefinitely and
mount an army of armed slaves. But Pendleton's
group is moving very slowly, in part because they
lack arms and men, in part because the majority is
conservative and cautious.

While they deliberate endlessly, the Capitol is
opened on October 14th for the beginning of the
fall General Assembly. It is hardly like other sessions. Not enough burgesses report to form a quo-
rum and the meeting is adjourned the same day.
The next session is set for spring but there isn't
too much optimism that it will be held.

Yet, even at this late date, many Virginians still
genuinely hope, if they do not positively believe,
that something can be done to turn back the clock
and resume the more than a century old alliance
with the mother country. This hope is reflected not
only in political circles but among the broad mass
of the people.

As recently as last month, Williamsburg learned
that the Lord Mayor, Aldermen, and Livery of London had addressed a petition to the King calling
for dismissal of all the ministers and Parliament.
The petition said, "We have already expressed to
your Majesty our abhorrence of the tyrannical

measures pursued against our fellow subjects in
America . . . we have seen with equal dread and
concern a civil war commenced in America by your
Majesty's commander-in-chief . . ." The words of
this petition bolster the hopes of the colonists, but
warlike deeds soon bring new doubts.

Lord Dunmore has turned his attention to the
village of Hampton, on the northern side of the
wide anchorage of Hampton Roads. Strongly anti-
British in feeling, Hampton is strategically located
and provides rebel access to the sea from Chesapeake Bay.

Recently, the town had been lost to the British
as a customs collection point for James River
traffic. Patriot forces had scuttled boats to block the
harbor entrance. So, on October 24th, Dunmore
dispatches ships under the command of Captain
Matthew Squire, the already infamous Hampton
Roads raider, to punish the unruly village.

That evening, Squire comes confidently to hook
with five vessels, anchoring them off the blockade
of scuttled boats. Immediately, he sends parties
ashore to loot.

Earlier in the month, a company of militia had
been sent from Williamsburg to Hampton, a distance of thirty miles, to augment the local volunteers and relieve them of garrison duty. Under the

command of Captain George Lyne, they are now eyeing the British from shore positions.

Gunfire echoes along Hampton Creek in the early morning hours as Captain Lyne engages two tenders from the banks in the first official clash involving patriot forces in Virginia. No damage is done since the shots from both sides splash short of the mark. But Captain Squire determinedly returns his men ashore to loot and burn outlying houses.

Sometime during this blustery, rainy evening, probably before midnight, Lyne dispatches a messenger to Williamsburg. Reaching the town, the messenger awakens Edmund Pendleton, relaying Lyne's appraisal of the situation.

Colonel William Woodford of Virginia's Second Regiment is ordered to the aid of Hampton with a company of Culpeper County's green-shirted men. They gallop out of town before daybreak in the continuing rain.

By now, in addition to his shore raiding, Squire has cut through the blockade of scuttled boats. Sometime after dawn, he maneuvers his five ships up the channel to draw abreast of Hampton for bombardment.

The British cannon begin to boom but within a few minutes Squire finds it a very risky operation.

The Woodford and Lyne patriots, hidden in buildings along the waterfront, discover that the cannon-loading British tars are much easier to hit than squirrels and rabbits, their usual targets in the piney woods and fields of Virginia.

Gunfire from the raiders slows and then stops. Squire shouts orders to get underway, but the process of raising sail is also uncomfortable as the patriots' long rifles pick off scrambling sailors. One British tender drifts ashore after being abandoned by its officers and men. Squire manages to get the other four vessels out of the now disastrous creek.

It is a minor victory for the patriots, but a victory nonetheless. Squirrel shot by citizen soldiers had driven back the cannon and musketry of His Majesty's Royal Navy. There is jubilation in Williamsburg as the news snakes through town.

Although the Committee of Safety has been working on plans to send troops after Dunmore's forces, simply to contain them, the brief battle at Hampton points up the need for action. The pressure increases when British vessels anchor within ten miles of College Landing, Williamsburg's "river port," practically within earshot of the committee. Although firing occurs now and then on the James this late October, it doesn't amount to much. A war of nerves best describes the situation.

There is even rumor afoot that the British plan to kidnap Martha Washington from Mount Vernon and hold her as hostage.

But the river sparring and the rumors are temporarily forgotten when the sad news arrives from Philadelphia that Peyton Randolph is dead. It is a blow to each of the colonies. For many in Williamsburg, it will seem strange not to see that round face and those heavy jowls in the hall of the House of Burgesses and not to feel his firm authority. Randolph's skill as a parliamentarian and a leader will be sorely missed in the days ahead. As "Mr. Speaker," chairman of all the Virginia conventions to date, and first president of the Continental Congress, he has served his people well. Going in and out of the shops and taverns and back and forth to his home on Market Square, Randolph always bore himself with great dignity. He will be remembered as one of the most admired men in the history of the town.

# 14 Battle of the Hogpen

Colonel Henry has suffered a setback. He has been bypassed. Edmund Pendleton's Committee of Safety has selected Colonel Woodford and the Second Regiment to do battle with Lord Dunmore in the Norfolk area, leaving the commander-in-chief to sit it out behind the college among the piles of moist autumn leaves beneath the bare trees.

It is a terrible blow to Henry's considerable pride. Not only was he not consulted when the decision was made to send Woodford to Norfolk, but Woodford's orders have been signed by seven of the eleven committee members and so written that he will not have to channel his communications through the now wing-clipped commander-in-chief. He will communicate directly to Pendleton and the committee and make his own battle decisions without reference to his superior.

Neither Henry nor Colonel Woodford are really qualified for the job. However, Woodford does have the tiny battle of Hampton Creek to his credit, in addition to some Indian combat. That he is a longtime close friend and a favorite of Pendleton is indicated by Pendleton's personal gift of "colours, drum and fife" to Woodford's Caroline Independents the previous year.

Then, too, Pendleton's opinion of Henry as a possible military leader is low. Also, the Committee of Safety is still dominated by conservatives. Giving Henry the splendid opportunity to make himself into a military hero was likely unthinkable in the gritty realism of politics.

So, while Colonel Henry, humiliated by the committee, smarts and broods in Williamsburg, Woodford crosses the James and marches his men down to the hamlet of Suffolk, a little west and south of Norfolk, on the lazy Nansemond River, well away from Dunmore's gunboats. Woodford plans to encamp there and await additional troops and artillery promised by North Carolina.

Troops under Lieutenant Colonel Charles Scott march on toward the crude fort that Lord Dunmore has built at Great Bridge, on the east branch of the sluggish Elizabeth, twelve miles south of Norfolk. Termed a "Hogpen," which it literally resembles, the fortification now controls that approach to the main Tidewater port, which is still a haven for Tories.

Scott throws up defenses at one end of the now dismantled "Great Bridge," which used to span the river, sealing off the muddy road that travels east. On the opposite bank of the river is a narrow causeway that leads up to the Hogpen, which has cannon mounted on its walls.

While Woodford awaits Colonel Robert Howe and his Carolinian support in Suffolk, Scott and his men daily eye the Hogpen over the pilings of the wrecked bridge. Reedy marshland lies along the river at this point. The bog is cold and damp, and the Shirtmen aren't exactly camped in style. Without dry straw to sleep on, the chill reaches into every bone at sundown.

With the opposing forces now facing each other, and battle probably inevitable, few people except the Tories are feeling sorry for Dunmore. On November 7th, he had issued a proclamation freeing the slaves and indentured servants, hoping to press them into his own service. If any patriot had the slightest sympathy for the plight of the governor and the Crown, this last proclamation, which also declared martial law in the colony, destroyed it. Like Massachusetts, Virginia was now under "military rule." Dunmore's order is meaningless, though, since the governor does not have the troops to enforce it.

Overshadowing Virginia's minor stabs at the governor's forces are the exploits of Vermont's militiamen, the "Green Mountain Boys," under Ethan Allen and Benedict Arnold. They had seized the British Fort Ticonderoga on Lake Champlain. Patriot soldiers had also captured Montreal, and Arnold has plans to advance to Quebec.

In Richmond, the Fourth Virginia Convention comes to order December 1, 1775, in an atmosphere not altogether friendly. Colonel Henry may be bottled up politically and militarily but his many supporters are active in venting their wrath at his treatment by Pendleton and the committee.

It is again a clash between the conservatives and the progressives.

Because of Dunmore's erratic nature, and the British raid at Hampton the past fall, Richmond had been chosen over Williamsburg as a safer place for the convention. But once the meeting is convened and Pendleton is selected as president, the delegates decide that they can return to the better accommodations offered in the capital. Dunmore is much too busy around Norfolk to disrupt the meeting.

Shifting the site doesn't solve the problem of Virginia's "commander-in-chief." In fact, it brings Henry's vocal supporters to within elbow distance of him. Additionally, Pendleton and his committee are in trouble over Woodford's stalling at Great Bridge. A few members of the committee are beginning to ridicule the colonel's inability to march on the fort, manned by only a few Redcoats and slaves.

Henry, meantime, is trying to get from Woodford information which "might be laid before the convention." He is needling Woodford but also trying desperately to gain some control of the expedition. By forcing Woodford to supply information to him personally, Henry can maintain some semblance of authority. Woodford thwarts him neatly by answering that his contact with Henry will be through the committee.

Although he has a superior number of troops, estimated at nine hundred, Woodford is worried about the fort's cannon. This is one reason for his stalling. Reaching the stockade also presents problems. With the bridge down, the only way to get to the Hogpen is to cross the Elizabeth River some five miles away and then attack the fort from a flank. Still without North Carolina's artillery, Woodford has only small arms to pit against the Hogpen cannon.

As of nightfall December 8th, Woodford, having moved from Suffolk a few days earlier to join Scott's group, is keeping his men in position behind the breastworks, hoping that Howe and his Carolina artillery will soon arrive. Men from Henry's regiment, minus their leader and unhappy, are also headed for Great Bridge, having been sent by Pendleton. When these units show up, Woodford plans to attack.

But the British don't wait. Sometime during the night they sneak out to place planks across the tops of the bridge pilings, forming temporary walkways to the rebel positions. At daybreak, regulars of the British Fourteenth Regiment, under

Captain Fordyce, move across the narrow causeway shoulder to shoulder, cannon fire falling ahead of them. Bayonets fixed, they advance steadily toward the planking.

Woodford is astonished. The British could well have stayed in the Hogpen and not exposed themselves to fire, thus forcing him to attack.

Sheltered behind their breastworks, the Shirtmen stop the Redcoats momentarily with their first volley. Fordyce forms his troops again and they advance courageously in the best tradition of His Majesty's army. The second patriot volley, from fifty yards away, takes a heavy toll, including Captain Fordyce.

The British retreat to the Hogpen, and the battle of Great Bridge, lasting about thirty minutes, is over. The citizen soldiers, with superb marksmanship, have won again and with ease.

During the night, as snow floats down, the battered British garrison abandons the fort and retreats to Norfolk, now a scene of frantic packing in loyalist houses. Tories are fleeing for their lives. With what belongings they can gather together quickly, they take to Dunmore's ships. Soon, some of Norfolk's previously most wealthy citizens are bobbing off the port in cramped quarters.

Woodford and Colonel Howe, who arrived with his North Carolina troops too late for the battle, plus three grousing companies from Henry's regiment, stay at Great Bridge until December 14th, and then march to Norfolk without opposition. On learning that he outranks Woodford, Howe takes command of the expedition, but joins with Woodford in sending a message to Williamsburg asking permission to burn Norfolk to prevent its further use as a British military base.

The delegates to the convention, having already cheered the victory over Dunmore on the Elizabeth's icy banks, ponder the new question, along with the military problems they have been debating for two weeks.

On January 1st, Lord Dunmore provides his own wrathful answer to the Woodford-Howe request. British bombardment of Norfolk begins on New Year's afternoon with a hundred guns booming out. Seeking vengeance, Dunmore hopes to destroy the port as a possible future base for rebel operations. Landing parties are sent ashore to fire buildings not already ablaze.

Within forty-eight hours, once proud Norfolk is almost in ashes, more than eight hundred buildings having been burned. When this news reaches

Williamsburg, the sometimes indecisive Committee of Safety is able to make up its mind. The complete destruction of the remaining four hundred buildings is ordered. Now, neither side can use the port.

The year 1776 arrives in Virginia Colony on crackling flames and billows of smoke.

# 15 The Lead in Great Affairs

On February 28, 1776, Colonel Henry is to appear before the Committee of Safety in Williamsburg to accept his new commission as colonel of the Continental Army, assigned to the Virginia First Battalion. Earlier in the month, the Continental Congress had incorporated the Virginia First and Second into a projected six regiments, appointing

Colonels Robert Howe and Andrew Lewis as brigadier generals in charge of the Virginia troops. The fighting men of each colony are being transferred into the national army under General Washington.

As Henry approaches Pendleton to read his new commission, he already knows that he has been outranked by two officers who were previously junior to him; that he is no longer commander-in-chief of Virginia forces, if he ever had been. He was denied the opportunity to fight the British at Great Bridge. He has been largely ignored by the Committee of Safety. His commission has turned out to be a galling "paper" title.

The move by the Continental Congress in replacing his command, undoubtedly a wise one, is a final crushing personal defeat for Henry. His burning ambition, perhaps both hopeless and foolish, to achieve military success to match his success as a statesman and politician has been permanently snuffed out. Henry declines the commission without presenting his reasons and leaves the room in complete silence.

In the *Journal of the Proceedings*, the committee comments almost as tersely:

Patrick Henry, Esquire, appeared in consequence of the letter wrote to him, and being offered his commission re-

ceived from the Continental Congress to be colonel of
the First Battalion declared he could not accept of same.

The affair of "soldier" Patrick Henry is over.
Obviously, some people were relieved that
Henry was no longer a leader in the military. Even
his ally and friend George Washington said later:
"I think my countrymen made a capital mistake,
when they took Henry out of the senate to place
him in the field . . ." Jefferson, too, later questioned Henry's ability as an officer. There were rumors that he could not maintain discipline.

Yet many of those who rallied to the side of
Pendleton in the dispute found it hard to condone
the methods used by the committee. Henry was denied the chance to carry out his appointed duties
and to test, even briefly, his ability. His performance might have been brilliant or catastrophic. No
one would ever know.

As word of Henry's resignation circulates
throughout the military forces in Williamsburg,
the immediate reaction is one of dismay. A group
of officers go to his lodgings to talk with him.
Ninety or so men draw up and present a testimo-
nial in which Henry is highly praised. After he replies to this memorial, they take him to an emo-
tional farewell dinner at the Raleigh Tavern.

Within the enlisted ranks this night there is

much talk of "demanding discharge" because of the treatment of the former commander-in-chief, some men flatly stating they will not serve under any other officer. Henry, now "Mister" again, seeks to calm the situation, replying that he has resigned "from motives in which his honor, alone," is concerned.

Briefly delaying his trip back to Hanover and his Scotchtown estate, he visits barracks and encampments, urging the men to stay in ranks. His popularity, despite the resignation, remains strong. So does his unpopularity with the Pendletonians.

Yet it almost seems that some inner flame in Henry has died in all this ruckus over a military rank. His pride wounded and his dream trampled, he leaves Williamsburg. People sense his hurt. He heads for Scotchtown the next day to take up responsibility for his six motherless children, Sarah having died the previous year after confinement for mental illness. There are stories that she became violent at times and had to be locked up in the basement.

Facing entirely different problems, and stung by public criticism, Pendleton soon writes Colonel Woodford: "The resignation of Colo. Henry has made much noise in the Countery, I believe from its not being understood. . . . It is said that Colo. Henry wanted to be a general & blames the Committee of Safety as having prevented him by their Solicitations to others. I can only say that as a Body they never mentioned the subject . . ."

Such was politics in Williamsburg.

Meanwhile, the neighboring colony of North Carolina has had its first formal battle of the war. On February 27th, patriot militia engaged a large force of Tories, under the command of General McDonald, at the Widow Moore's creek bridge not far from Wilmington, routing the British partisans in less than five minutes. The undeclared war has spread throughout the colonies.

March arrives, colder and damper than usual, but with a warmer climate of public opinion, for Tom Paine's vigorous pamphlet *Common Sense* has hit town. The pamphlet advocates "Independence and a Continental form of government," ideas that seem to many to make good sense indeed.

Virginia's political leaders are mostly at home. Jefferson is in residence in his mountaintop home, Monticello, across the Rivanna River near Shadwell. He's looking after personal business following his long stay in Philadelphia. Plagued by headaches this spring, he isn't looking forward to making the journey back to Quaker City for the next round of congressional meetings.

Still deeply concerned with the Committee of Safety's pressing problems in raising troops and supplying them, and still keeping a watchful eye on Lord Dunmore's ships, Pendleton is in Williamsburg but has plans to return to his home, Edmundsbury plantation, in Carolina County. He would like to survey the spring planting before the start of Virginia's Fifth Convention. Increasingly important since the collapse of British rule, these meetings permit the delegates to relay the desires of the people in their home counties, and allow the governing of the colony to be carried on.

Up at Gunston Hall, on Pohick Creek, George Mason is again suffering from stabs of gout, that painful inflammation of the joints said to be caused by too much rich food and strong drink. Mason is a lover of both. Fretting about money matters, he is also very much aware that he's up for election to the Fifth Convention as a delegate from Fairfax County. Thus far he's avoided public office, except for a term as a burgess in 1759, and earlier a justice of the peace.

Before blustery March is struck from the calendar in Dr. Pasteur's apothecary shop, General

Charles Lee arrives to take over as commander of the Southern Department of the Continental Army. Dispatched by Washington from the Boston area, the shabbily dressed former British officer makes his entrance in a driving rainstorm.

Lord William Howe, who had replaced General Gage, and his Redcoats had retreated from their long occupation of Boston. Washington's siege had forced them out. General Lee could now be spared to mold the southern forces against attack. Almost certainly they would be launched.

Skinny, with a big nose and a reputation for a violent temper, and usually followed by a pack of mangy dogs, Lee is often seen around town. Washington has great confidence in him but admits to his bobcat temper and instability. The swaggering Britisher is quite unlike the gentlemanly Pendleton, with whom he'll have to deal.

On April 2nd, George Mason takes note of Howe's departure from Boston in a letter to Washington: "We have just received the welcome news of your having, with so much address and success, dislodged the Ministerial Troops and taken possession of the town of Boston. I congratulate you most heartily upon this glorious and important event . . ."

Actually, after a savage winter, with patriot soldiers freezing from lack of clothing, shelter, and firewood, some even deserting, Howe's retreat to Halifax, Nova Scotia, is more important as a boost to the colonists' spirits than as a victory in military strategy.

Yet, thus far, and remarkably, the patriots have won more battles than they have lost.

April is the month when the first tender shoots show on the oaks and weeping willows, when the plows begin to slide through the good, wet earth. This April of 1776 is also a time for the blossoming of the spirit of independence.

Despite the many incidents of the past—the protests against the Stamp Act, the turmoil in Boston, the fiery speeches of Patrick Henry, the battles of Lexington and Concord and Bunker Hill—relatively few Virginians have honestly and seriously considered taking the final step until this very spring. Always, they have hoped for a reconciliation with England. Now, the clear majority of the people seem to favor a complete break with the mother country.

The dispute between England and the colonies can be compared to a family fight. The colonists are like growing children, desirous of independence, yet bound by ancient ties, somewhat fearful of going out into the world alone. Those who still cannot contemplate such a drastic step are now in a minority.

After the British burning of Norfolk and Falmouth, Massachusetts, Washington had read Citizen Paine's *Common Sense* and had written: "A few more such flaming arguments as were exhibited at Falmouth and Norfolk, added to the sound doctrine and unanswerable reasoning contained in the pamphlet 'Common Sense' will not leave numbers at loss to decide upon the propriety of separation."

Clear signs of unity appear in Virginia and nearby colonies. On April 12th, the North Carolina Provincial Congress, meeting in Halifax near the Virginia border, takes the first definite step toward independence. The congress passes resolutions instructing North Carolina's delegates to the Second Continental Congress at Philadelphia to join the other delegates and vote for separation. That same day John Page, Jefferson's close friend and former fellow student at William and Mary, claims that almost every man in Virginia is willing to break away from England.

Exactly a week later, Virginia elects its delegates to the Fifth Convention, to be held in Williamsburg beginning May 6th. Many are given flat instructions to rebel against the Crown.

Cumberland County tells its delegates John Mayo and William Fleming: "We, therefore, your constituents, instruct you positively to declare for independence, that you solemnly abjure any allegiance to his Brittanick Majesty . . ."

Charlotte County tells Paul Carrington and Thomas Read: "We give it to you to use your best endeavors that the delegates which are sent to the General Congress be instructed immediately to cast off the British yoke . . ."

Patrick Henry returns again to public life as a delegate from Hanover County, where rancor still simmers over the Committee of Safety's actions concerning his military career. He wins the election without trouble.

Letters flow to and from Philadelphia.

On April 20th, Richard Henry Lee, already in Philadelphia for the Second Continental Congress, writes to Henry: "Virginia has hitherto taken the lead in great affairs and many look to her now with anxious expectations . . . ages yet unborn and millions existing at present may rue or bless the assembly on which their happiness or misery so eminently depends." Lee is urging Henry to carry on the fight for independence.

Thomas Jefferson surveyed the northern counties of Virginia near Monticello and found that nine-tenths of the people now wanted to cut the ties with England. He had suspected this was the case, but felt he should go out to the people and talk with them to be sure. Soon he departs for Philadelphia with his usual companion, a slave named Bob.

Two letters await him in that city. One is from Thomas Nelson, Jr.: "The notion of independency seems to spread fast in this colony, and will be adopted, I dare say, by the majority of the next convention." He is referring to the Virginia Fifth, upcoming.

The other letter is from John Page and very much to the point: "For God's sake, declare the colonies independent and save us from ruin."

# 16 A Town Awakens

As Williamsburg stirs and cooking fires are lit, oak smoke begins to coil up from the chimneys. Soon it will be mingled with the smell of breakfast as men, emerging from their crowded sleeping accommodations in the taverns, inns, and boarding-houses, roll out to start what promises to be an eventful morning.

Delegates from all over Virginia are present. It is May 6, 1776, opening day of the Fifth Convention, as well as the day to convene the General Assembly. Some predict that the House of Burgesses, that once noble governing body, will cease to exist within hours. Whatever happens to the burgesses, fifty crucial days lie ahead.

Already up, or soon to arise, are Patrick Henry and Edmund Pendleton. Most of the other one hundred and twenty-eight delegates are also in Williamsburg or riding toward it in the abnormal chill.

The past two days have seen bleak clouds and steady downpours. Some of the horses and riders are spattered with red clay. Wagon and carriage wheels are crusted with mud. After the winter rains, deep frosts, and snows, the roads leading to town are in worse shape than usual. But the dogwood is in bloom again, its shimmering ivory petals announcing that warm days will soon arrive.

Some of the delegates from distant counties have been on horseback for a week, their wooden trunks lashed to trailing pack animals. These delegates, in from the wilderness, are always armed. They don't worry about the British as much as the possibility of Indian attack.

They have ridden over pine-studded mountains

and forded swift, clear streams where herring and sturgeon explode in twisting runs. They've ferried wide rivers like the James or splashed across smaller ones like the Chickahominy or Mattaponi, Indian names that always amaze travelers from Europe. They've been determined to reach Williamsburg in time for the start of proceedings. They know that the other colonies have either already held their conventions or will assemble shortly.

In the northern city of Philadelphia, Virginia's representatives to the Second Continental Congress, Richard Henry Lee, George Wythe, and Thomas Jefferson, among others, are anxiously awaiting the actions to be taken in Williamsburg. Will the delegates vote to declare independence from England?

Soon the burgesses who have already arrived begin to gather in the Capitol. Most of them are also delegates to the Fifth Convention. Quickly it becomes apparent that the General Assembly is dead. No session has been held since June past when it was convened by Lord Dunmore, but he's hardly in a position this spring to sanction an Assembly, dissolve it, or disrupt it. Undoubtedly seething at the thought of what is transpiring less than a mile from his former palace, he's still aboard the British man-of-war off Norfolk.

Only thirty-two burgesses report and the *Journal of Proceedings* notes:

> Several members met, but did not proceed to business, nor adjourn, as a House of Burgesses.
>
> Finis.

And that, pitifully, was all that was said at this final session of the 168-year-old Virginia General Assembly.

But now the Fifth Convention can get underway in this same hall. Just outside the door is a comparatively recent statue of the late and beloved Governor Botetourt. In the stance of an orator, the marble nobleman looks down on the small lobby. An inscription on one side of the base of the statue reads: "Let wisdom and justice preside in any Country. The people will rejoice and be happy"— good advice on this day.

Of course, in the eyes of Lord Dunmore, George III, and the British Parliament, this convention and the congress in Philadelphia are scandalous, illegal, rebellious gatherings without the slightest authority. Actually, whatever Dunmore or the king's gardener or all of England thinks about either revolutionary body is of little consequence to the colonists, and arguments about the legality of the two bodies are useless. Nothing short of an army could stop the men from holding their meetings.

Most of the faces in the hall of the Capitol are very familiar. Edmund Pendleton is once more favored to assume leadership of the convention, and Patrick Henry is back again to give him opposition. Their relationship remains polite but cold. There is no reason to believe that they will not clash again and again.

The oldest delegate is sixty-six-year-old Richard Bland, who has been in Virginia politics for thirty years. Nearly blind, he moves slowly and uncertainly in the increasing babble.

A rich, influential Randolph has always held high office, and among the young men in the hall is Edmund Randolph, twenty-three years old, the delegate from the City of Williamsburg. His father, John, the loyalist attorney general under Dunmore, has made good his threat and returned to England rather than be a part of the rebellion. But Edmund has other ideas and happens to be in sympathy with most Virginians. He will be Jefferson's spokesman here.

Another inexperienced young man is twenty-five-year-old James Madison, a newly elected delegate from Orange County. Studious and shy, he is destined to be the fourth president of the United States. Young Madison, in particular, is anticipating the sight and sound of Patrick Henry. He's heard much about Henry but has never seen him.

The man who is most likely to fight independence to the last moment of debate is also present, Robert Carter Nicholas. No one yet has convinced this delicately featured blueblood that it is wise to break the few remaining bonds with England.

One extremely important delegate is missing. Colonel George Mason is still at home at Gunston Hall, complaining of gout pains. It is reported that he'll ride to Williamsburg as soon as his joints stop acting up.

Although the progressives and liberals, led again by Mr. Henry, now wield enough power and can summon enough votes to sway the convention, little has changed in the past ten years. Their every action will be contested by the conservatives even though both groups are basically in agreement on the main issue of independence.

Though Henry seems to have lost some of his fire, his talent for inciting emotions has not dimmed. Before the year is out, conservative delegate Colonel Archibald Cary, a planter and horse breeder from Chesterfield County, will reportedly threaten to plunge a dagger into the Hanover heart if Mr. Henry tries to "be a dictator." Cary fears Henry's power to incite the people.

As the sound of shuffling feet dies away and the babble begins to end, there is justifiable speculation as to what the Hanover delegate will do and say in the weeks ahead.

# 17 The Interesting Question of Independence

The delegates to the Fifth Virginia Convention are now all seated and the hall is silent. Gone forever are the squabbles with British governors, and the annoying orders for the General Assembly to dissolve prematurely; gone are Fauquier's benign smiles, Botetourt's grand entry in a suitcoat of gold cloth, Peyton Randolph's calm and dignified presence, Dunmore's glower, and Henry's startling words, "Caesar has his Brutus . . ." But the memory of them is embedded in this hall of the House of Burgesses where England's former Queen Caroline still looks down from her portrait with wistful eyes.

Today, however, what must be considered is the future of the colony, perhaps of a nation, and the faces of the delegates are expectant.

As the first order of business, John Tazewell is again elected clerk. Then it is time to nominate the president, and no one is surprised when Richard Bland, wearing a green eyeshade, rises up slowly, showing his age, to place Edmund Pendleton's name before the delegates. In a short speech, he praises Pendleton as a man of ability and integrity; the nomination is quickly seconded by "Old Iron," Colonel Archibald Cary.

It is obvious that the conservatives are hoping for a unanimous vote on Pendleton's presidency. No wrangling or opposition. If the convention is to lead the way in affairs for Virginia, as well as for other colonies, solidarity is needed. But the events of the past winter and Patrick Henry's alleged mistreatment by Mr. Pendleton and the Committee of Safety are not easily forgotten.

So Thomas Johnson of Louisa County takes the

opportunity to show the progressives' displeasure by rising to place a Henry ally, Thomas Ludwell Lee, from Stafford County, before the convention. Lee had been a progressive member of Pendleton's committee, generally opposed to its cautiousness, and one of those who had sharply criticized Woodford's stalling at Great Bridge.

There are murmurs of disgust from the conservatives but the nomination is seconded. Mr. Henry sits with a poker face as the clash between the conservatives and the liberals is again joined before the benches are even warm.

Clerk Tazewell puts the question to the floor and Edmund Pendleton becomes president by a narrow margin. The Henry faction goes down to defeat as the conservatives and moderates combine votes in the same old seesaw battle.

Bland and Cary conduct the tall, distinguished statesman, still handsome at the age of fifty-four, to the high-backed chair, where the ghost of Peyton Randolph seems to linger on. Standing before it, Pendleton begins to address the convention:

"Gentlemen, be pleased to accept my sincere thanks for the honour done me in your election to this high and important office. . . . We are now met in General Convention according to the ordinance for our election, at a time truly critical, when subjects of the most important and interesting nature require our serious attention."

His voice is even and solemn. If any of those in the gallery were expecting fireworks, some exciting patriotic message that would cause everyone to dash out into the street, they must have been disappointed.

Pendleton speaks rather matter-of-factly for about four minutes, talking of the need to try criminal and political cases (no courts had met for more than a year), of Virginia's military requirements, and of resolutions from the Continental Congress that awaited action. Nowhere does he specifically mention that "interesting question" of independence. Perhaps it is wise; nonetheless, some are disappointed.

Pendleton concludes his speech by saying, "In discussion of these, and all other subjects which may come under our consideration, permit me to recommend calmness, unanimity and diligence, as the most likely means of bringing them to a happy and prosperous issue." Perhaps he is speaking, indirectly, to Mr. Henry and his followers, not always practitioners of calmness.

Then the convention proceeds into the usual routines of opening day. A chaplain, the Reverend Thomas Price, is selected, and he is ordered to read his prayers at 9 A.M.; four doorkeepers are appointed to maintain order. Some resolutions of little importance are read. Finally, Pendleton adjourns the meeting until 10 A.M. the following day.

For the beginning of an event that might affect "ages yet unborn," it has been curiously humdrum and dull, aside from the small hubbub over Thomas Ludwell Lee's nomination. Just what had happened to the fever of rebellion? Mr. Pendleton had said nothing about breaking with England; Mr. Henry had hardly moved his lips.

Strangely enough, the next day, Tuesday, it appears that Mr. Henry now has some doubts about an "immediate" declaration of independence. For him to take on overnight the cloak of caution is puzzling indeed. From the very day he stepped into this hall, even before when he defended the Parson's Cause, he has been challenging British rule.

He's still strongly in favor of separation but on this eve of decision he has apparently had second thoughts and would now like to see the colonies united in a form of government *prior to separation.* He would also prefer that the colonies form an alliance with France and Spain before the break. The new nation will need aid from known friends. Richard Henry Lee raised these points in his letter of April 20th. They are now troubling Mr. Henry, the man who has sometimes plunged recklessly, devil taking the hindmost.

What seems to be shaping up in Williamsburg, if one listens to lobby, street, and tavern talk, is an immediate move to send Virginia out alone, acting independently of the other colonies. Virginia will break with England without certain knowledge that the other colonies will follow suit, without a form of government, and without known foreign allies. Perhaps the enormity of this step has, at last, put brakes on the Virginia radical.

Henry's thoughts had surfaced in a conversation with General Charles Lee on Monday. Lee wanted to sever relations with England immediately. A month earlier, the new leader of the southern Continental Army had written the Virginia delegates in Philadelphia to say, "For God's sakes, why do you dandle in congress so strangely? Why do you not at once declare yourselves a separate independent state?"

On Tuesday, Lee again attempted to convince the single delegate least expected to waver. He penned a note to Henry: "Since our conversation yesterday, my thoughts have been solely employed on that great question. . . . You say, and with great justice, that we ought previously to have felt the pulse of France and Spain. I more than believe,

I am almost confident it has been done. . . . In this persuasion, I most devoutly pray that you do not merely recommend, but positively lay injunctions on your servants in Congress to embrace a measure so necessary to our salvation."

Pendleton had earlier advanced his own questions about an immediate separation, and the colorful, brash Lee had written General Washington that Pendleton's arguments would have disgraced "an old midwife drunk with bohea tea and gin."

But as Henry ponders the general's note from his new and surprising position as an advocate of caution, a position sharply different from the "Why stand we here idle?" speech of St. John's Church, the convention goes on about its work.

The committees, their number constantly growing, often begin their sessions on the second floor of the Capitol at 7 A.M., three hours before the entire convention assembles if it is to meet as a whole. In fact, the Reverend Price is ordered to say his blessings at seven rather than nine so that the delegates can be off to an early start. Breakfast at the taverns and inns can be obtained at six.

Aside from a dinner recess about five, and a little "refreshment" of wine or rum at the King's Arms or the Raleigh, the delegates are at work by candle glow in the committee rooms until nine or ten, six days a week. Even mealtime recesses are occasions to hammer at problems. The committees, numbering fourteen eventually, range from one on methods to encourage the manufacture of "salt, saltpeter and gunpowder" to others on hospital construction and punishments for "enemies of America in this colony."

By design, the subject of independence does not erupt on the floor of the Capitol for the remainder of the opening week, though everyone is talking about it in committee meetings, in taverns, and on the streets of Williamsburg. It seems as if the delegates are postponing the debate as one is apt to postpone an unpleasant job. Their reluctance is noted by Alexander Purdie, the public printer and a staunch patriot. An enterprising man, he sells books, stationery, and music for harpsichord, but the hot item this day, May 11th, as the delegates adjourn for the weekend, is his newspaper. On the front page, they can read the following:

It is not a time to trifle. Men who know they deserve nothing from their country & whose hope is on the arm that hath sought to enslave us, may hold to you, as "Cato" [a Tory writer] hath done, the false light of reconciliation. There is no such thing. Tis gone! Tis past! The grave hath parted us! Death in the persons of the slain hath cut the thread between Britain and America.

# 18 May 15th: A Declaration of Independence

For more than seventy years, in clear weather and foul, the proud flag of the British Empire has been flying at the east end of Duke of Gloucester Street. It is again two-blocked on the white pole above the Capitol this Tuesday morning, May 14th.

Word has gone through town that the delegates will finally meet as a Committee of the Whole to discuss independence. People are streaming toward the Capitol and standing about in the brick-pathed yard.

Some citizens and some delegates glance up toward the flag. For so flimsy a thing, the British flag has massive weight behind it. It represents the wealth and military might of a long established nation. It represents the greatest single power on earth. Yet, as the delegates move up the walk, under the graceful arches, and into the lobby, they know that no matter how powerful England is, all "trifling" with the question of independence has come to an end.

The gallery is solid with spectators and all of the elected delegates are present except George Mason, still wrestling with gout on Pohick Creek.

After the convention comes to order, the chair recognizes Colonel Meriwether Smith. Nicknamed "Fiddlehead," Smith is a planter from Essex County on the Rappahannock River. His lands are subject to easy attack from the water by the British. Nonetheless, he sides with the majority of men in the hall; he is ready for the final step. But his thinking is conservative and so is his resolution:

> That the government of this colony as hitherto exercised under the Crown of Great Britain be dissolved, and

that a committee be appointed to prepare a Declaration of Rights and such a Plan of Government, as shall be judged most proper to maintain Peace and Order in this colony, and secure substantial and equal liberty to the people.

It is not strong enough. *Independence* is not mentioned, and the government, as it existed in the past, has already dissolved itself. The General Assembly is no more and the British governor has fled. Smith has not specifically recommended a complete break with England.

Robert Carter Nicholas rises. His first words indicate he'll fight to the last breath to save the colony for the Crown. The delegates listen but are not impressed.

By this time Patrick Henry has thought it all over and has decided on a course of action. Whatever doubts he had expressed to General Lee and others during the first week of the convention have been overcome. He now believes that the prudent course is to declare himself strongly for independence and then hope that his other ideas will be considered.

In the preamble to his resolution, the next submitted, he calls King George III a "tyrant" and claims that "Parliament is making every preparation to crush us." He points out that the "humble petitions of the Continental Congress [have] been rejected and treated with contempt." These petitions, calling for an end to the oppression of the colonies, had been sent to England the previous fall.

In fact, he almost sounds like the fiery, positive Mr. Henry of 1775 in proposing that:

> We, the representatives of the colony of Virginia, do declare ourselves absolved of all allegiances to the Crown of Great Britain and obliged by the eternal laws of self-preservation to pursue such measures as may conduce to the good and happiness of the united colonies; and as a full Declaration of Independency appears to be the only honourable means under Heaven of obtaining that happiness, and restoring us again to a tranquil and prosperous situation—Resolved, That our delegates to Congress be enjoined in the strongest and most positive manner to exert their ability to procure an immediate, clear and full Declaration of Independence.

At last, it has been said—and with power.

There is a stir in the hall; some nod their heads in approval. The resolution does not call for a plan of government, nor for the drawing up of a bill of rights, but deals firmly and squarely with separation. The convention now has a choice between the soft and rather vague resolution of Meriwether Smith and Henry's direct proposal.

A third resolution, authored by Pendleton, is submitted. Its main point is:

> That the union that has hitherto subsisted between Great Britain and the American colonies is thereby dissolved and that the inhabitants of this colony are discharged from any allegiance to the crown of Great Britain.

It is stronger than Smith's but weaker than Henry's.

Robert Carter Nicholas goes on the attack again. The wealthy lawyer and politician is beside himself as the resolutions are read. All this day, off and on, he protests. The delegates listen but few change their minds. Finally, at about five o'clock, Pendleton calls for adjournment.

There has been enough debate to expose the general viewpoints of the delegates. Of the three roughly written resolves, only Henry's makes an outright bid for independence. Yet, at the same time, the three viewpoints are not that far apart. The differences are a matter of wording. Edmund Pendleton takes the resolutions with him to his inn and sometime after dinner sits down at a writing desk to draft a new proposal, drawing on the Smith and Henry resolutions as well as his own.

The Fifth Convention was to meet in Williamsburg for fifty days, and there has long been argument about which of the days was most important in the shaping of the history of the United States. Very likely it was Wednesday, May 15th.

Pendleton had labored over his draft of the new resolution during the night and he brings it with him to the Capitol in the morning, giving it to Colonel Cary to introduce. "Old Iron" is recognized and submits the resolution soon after the hall is called to order.

Following a long and rambling preface, which does not reflect Pendleton's usual skill as a writer, are these words:

> That the delegates appointed to represent this colony in General Congress be instructed to propose to that respectable body to declare the United Colonies free and independent states. . . .

A ripple of excitement goes through the hall. Pendleton, so long the moderate, is now going beyond the resolutions of Smith and Henry. He is not speaking for Virginia alone but for all the colonies, calling them "united" even now.

Also in the resolution is a recommendation that the colonies form foreign alliances, and that a confederation of the colonies be established, though each colony is to be left free to form its own government. The colonies are to be "states," governed by themselves though united with each other.

A second resolution Pendleton has prepared provides that a committee be appointed to prepare a Declaration of Rights, detailing human freedoms in a free society, and a Plan of Government for the colony.

It is a sweeping work that Cary introduces. It is almost as if Pendleton had said to himself, as he sat writing at his desk, "If we go, we shall go all the way." The proposals satisfy the progressives beyond their greatest hopes.

Either during the evening, or at breakfast, or possibly just before the session convened on the 15th, Pendleton got together with Thomas Nelson, Jr., the chunky aristocratic delegate from York County, and Patrick Henry to assure passage of the resolutions against the certain opposition of Nicholas. Nelson is to stand in support of Pendleton's proposals first, to be followed by Patrick Henry. At last, the two patriots, Pendleton and Henry, though enemies to their graves, are united for the good of the colony and the country.

The combination of Nelson and Henry is masterful. Their backgrounds are very different, as are the voters they represent. Yet they are of one mind concerning England. Nelson, along with Thomas Jefferson, had sprung to the immediate support of Henry the past year at St. John's.

Mr. Nelson speaks briefly in behalf of the Pen-

dleton resolutions, and then, according to plan, Mr. Henry is recognized. He rises from his place, pays his respects to President Pendleton, and acknowledges the assembled delegates; then he begins his speech.

It is the Patrick Henry of old, the orator of Hanover Courthouse and the serene white church above Shockoe Creek; his speech is spellbinding. Complete silence descends on the hall as the words pour out.

Much later, Edmund Randolph recalls: "As a pillar of fire, which, notwithstanding the darkness of the prospect would lead to the promised land, he inflamed and was followed by the convention. His eloquence unlocked the secret strings of the human heart, robbed danger of all its terror, and broke the keystone in the arch of royal power."

After Mr. Henry sits down, to loud applause, the resolutions are read twice again and then the call to vote is issued. They pass unanimously, all one hundred and twelve delegates present voting in the affirmative, including a dejected Robert Carter Nicholas.

So, on May 15, 1776, Virginia becomes the first colony to instruct its delegates flatly to declare it freed from England. North Carolina and Rhode Island had directed their delegates to *concur* with the other colonies on the subject, but seemed reluctant to take the final step independently.

Within minutes after Clerk Tazewell finishes the roll call and the vote becomes official, spectators run outside to see the doorkeepers haul down the British flag from the Capitol cupola. It is a strange moment; only minutes before, the spectators had all been British subjects. Then, as the "Continental" flag goes up, the cheers resound.

Yet there is no great jubilation or tumult within the Capitol itself as a rather sober body of the people's representatives completes the work of the day. Pendleton immediately names a committee to begin drafting the Declaration of Rights.

Perhaps it is always this way with great decisive moments. They come quietly. Celebration begins afterward.

A celebration will take place, to be sure, for before the convention adjourns in the afternoon, hats are being passed through the hall to collect money to "entertain the troops." The money will buy food, ale, and rum.

One very pleased gentleman, Thomas Nelson, Jr., an alternate delegate to the Continental Congress, prepares to ride for the Quaker City. He will hand to Richard Henry Lee a copy of the resolutions instructing Virginia's delegates to declare for independence. Hopefully, the men from Virginia will lead the way toward a declaration of independence by the Congress itself.

Meanwhile, word flashes around Williamsburg that the delegates have chosen freedom for the people. For proof, all anyone has to do is look down Duke of Gloucester Street and see the new flag flying above the Capitol.

# 19 To the American Independent States

The next day, Thursday, little time is spent in politicking. It is a holiday in Williamsburg and the mood is happy, optimistic. The delegates pass a motion to adjourn until Saturday, setting aside Friday as "Congress Sunday," a day of fasting and religious services. Then they walk to Waller's Grove, beyond the Capitol, where the troops are gathered for ceremonies.

Most of Williamsburg is there, too. Shops are closed. The college has suspended classes. Men, women, and children, black and white, have thronged to Waller's Grove.

The soldiers are ill-clad and ill-equipped, but as they parade before the Committee of Safety, the convention delegates, and Brigadier General Andrew Lewis, they seem to be in high spirits. The thin notes of the fifes cleave the spring air and the drumbeats are determined.

After the men pass in review and reform in ranks, the resolutions, now on their way to Philadelphia in Colonel Nelson's saddlebag, are read. Toasts are shouted:

"To the American Independent States."

"To the Grand Congress of the United States, and their respective legislatures."

After each toast, Captain Arundel's artillery booms, echoing across Williamsburg. The acrid smell of burnt powder is good this day.

Purdie's *Gazette* of May 17th sums it up:

> The Union Flag of the American States waved upon the Capitol during the whole of the ceremony; which being ended, the soldiers partook of refreshments prepared for them by the affections of their countrymen, and the evening concluded with illuminations, and other demonstrations of joy; everyone seeming pleased that the domination of Great Britain was now at end . . .

Readers of the May 17th edition can also see that the British seal has disappeared from the masthead of the paper. In its place is the motto "United We Stand—Divided We Fall."

The people of the town go home in the early evening past bonfires and candles glowing in windows. After so many years, Williamsburg is no longer the seat of an overseas colonial government. It is now a place within the new "American States" as the *Gazette* is quick to note, though a bit prematurely.

On Friday, "Congress Sunday," the delegates assemble at the Capitol, and then march slowly toward Bruton Church. The sergeant at arms, carrying the silver mace, is in the lead, followed by Mr. Pendleton, finely robed, and then the members.

The Reverend Price calls out from the pulpit, "Hearken ye, all Judah! Be not afraid, nor dismayed, by reason of this great multitude, for the battle is not yours, but God's."

The multitude to which he is referring are the estimated forty-five thousand British and German troops reportedly sailing for America.

# 20 The Squire of Gunston Hall

Patrick Henry's hour in history has passed. He has served his purpose and the cause of the people brilliantly. In the years to come, some will try to tarnish his name and role, to write him off as a reckless rabble-rouser and a man of small vision and shallow thought. But with his spirit and matchless oratory, he reached masses of people and gave them conviction. He provided the early inner flame of revolution.

For Colonel George Mason, arriving in Williamsburg this solemn afternoon of May 17th, in the midst of fasting and prayer, a new role is just beginning. It is time to set the course of a government, time for inspired thinking and writing.

Fifty years old, nearly six feet tall, Mason is another of the many physically striking Virginians who gathered for this convention. His black hair is ticked with gray; his black eyes are half-sad, half-severe. His bearing is as aristocratic as his position in society, but he dislikes the chains of monarchy and the hidebound approaches of men like Bland and Nicholas.

Though he is not a lawyer, his knowledge of law and constitution is vast. He has studied the political history of England, the charters of the colonies, and the British constitution. He has long had a reputation for clear thought and good judgment.

Only events of great importance have ever lured him away from the good life at Gunston Hall, with its deer park and orchards, its tobacco fields, and its cherry trees—now in full blossom—which line the roadways to the mansion. The plantation is a village in itself with its own weavers and shoemakers and tanners. There is little need to travel, for almost everything is available at Gunston Hall.

But Mason has never held back in times of crisis. During the commotion over the Stamp Act, he wrote a letter of sharp warning to the British public, and said of himself: "These are the sentiments of a man who spends most of his time in retirement and has seldom meddled in public affairs; who enjoys a modest but independent fortune, and content with the blessing of a private station, equally disregards the smiles and favors of the great."

As the convention resumes on May 18th, Mason's value is immediately recognized. He is placed on the four most important committees: Declaration of Rights and Plan of Government, Propositions and Grievances, Privileges and Elections, and the committee to establish ways to manufacture gunpowder. So on this Saturday, he is the most sought-after man at the convention.

Sometime during the day he finds a few minutes to write to Richard Henry Lee in Philadelphia: "Dear Sir—After a smart fit of gout, which detained me at home the first of the session, I have at last reached this place, where, to my great satisfaction, I find the first grand point has been carried

. . . the opponents being so few that they did not think fit to divide or contradict the general voice. . . . The Committee appointed to prepare a plan [of government] is, according to custom, over-charged with useless members. We shall, in all probability, have a thousand ridiculous and imprac-ticable proposals . . . and of course a plan formed of unintelligible ingredients. This can be prevented only by a few men of integrity and abilities, whose country's interest lies next to their hearts, under-taking this business and defending it ably through every stage of opposition . . ."

Already, he is viewing the undertaking with a harsh sense of reality. It is not surprising that Mason is selected to be the committee's chief draftsman of Virginia's Declaration of Rights.

On Monday, the bulky, "overcharged" commit-tee of thirty-two men, under the chairmanship of Colonel Cary, begins work on the document. Its members include Patrick Henry at one extreme and Robert Carter Nicholas at the other; the pro-gressive James Madison is a late addition. But it is Mason's pen that will do the chief work. From this committee will come not only a plan of govern-ment, to replace the government administered by the British, but a declaration by Virginia of the rights of all men.

Some say that Mason began writing the Declaration of Rights in his room at the Raleigh Tavern. Others claim it was done in preliminary form at Gunston Hall on a walnut table, with a copy of the Magna Carta, the "great charter" of English liberties of A.D. 1215, and other European expressions of political thought and liberty at his fingertips.

Wherever the early work was done, whatever thought Mason put into the task prior to this week, the document is being forged in Williamsburg, in the committee room at the Capitol and in Mason's room at the Raleigh. As Mason had predicted, the committee members are coming up with a "thousand ridiculous and impracticable proposals." Each is argued.

A year earlier, at the election of officers of the Independent Company of Fairfax County, Mason had read a paper he'd written. In part, it said:

> We came equals into this world and equals we shall go out. All men are by nature equally free and independent. To protect the weaker from the injuries and insults of the stronger were societies first formed. . . . Every society, all governments, and every kind of civil compact therefore, is or ought to be, calculated for the general good and safety of the community. . . .

These thoughts are becoming the basis of Virginia's Declaration of Rights. As Mason's pen moves, by day or by the pale flickers of candle at night, the noise and laughter of the Raleigh welling up from below, the articles take form and substance:

Article II—That all Power is vested in, and consequently derived from the people. . . .

Article III—That Government is, or ought to be, instituted for the common Benefits, Protection and Security of all the People. . . .

Article IV—That no Man, or Set of Men, are entitled to exclusive or separate Emoluments or Privileges from the Community. . . .

The words flow on. Mason is influenced, very likely, by one or another member of the committee, but the document is largely his work: *Right to jury trial; freedom of the press; free exercise of religion.* Later, claims would be made that Patrick Henry constructed two of the articles, Madison one. Perhaps they did, but there is no proof.

Some fear that the usual contest between the progressives and the conservatives will take place over both the Declaration of Rights and the plan of government (constitution), soon to be written by the same committee. But such a contest is healthy, as both sets of partisans fight to place their viewpoints in both documents.

On May 20th, Henry writes to Richard Henry

Lee in Philadelphia: "The grand work of forming the constitution in Virginia is now before the convention, where your love of equal liberty and your skill in public counsels might so eminently serve the cause of your country. Perhaps I'm mistaken, but I fear too great a bias of aristocracy prevails among the opulent. Vigor, animation and all the powers of the mind and body must now be summoned and collected together in one grand effort. Moderation, falsely so called, hath nearly brought on us final ruin . . ."

The same day Henry writes to John Adams, a Massachusetts delegate to the Continental Congress, "Would to God you and Sam Adams were here."

Henry's concern that the Declaration of Rights and the constitution will be watered down by the conservatives is shared by Mason, Thomas Ludwell Lee, and others. Doubtless there will be floor battles after the documents are introduced to the full convention. The hot arguments in committee between the progressives and Nicholas, Cary, and Bland continue.

Pendleton is staying aloof of the battling and on May 24th writes to Jefferson in Philadelphia: "The Political Cooks are busy preparing the dish. . . . I find our session will be a long one and indeed the importance of our business requires it & we must sweat it out with Fortitude." A week later, he sends another report to Jefferson: ". . . We build a government slowly. I hope it will be founded on rock."

On May 27th Colonel Nelson finally arrives in Philadelphia with Virginia's resolve to declare independence. The document is handed over to Richard Henry Lee, George Wythe, and Jefferson. Nelson stays on in the Quaker City, now heating up to become a humid furnace in June and July. He is an alternate to Lee, who has plans to return to Williamsburg to comfort his ailing wife.

On this same day in Virginia's capital, Colonel Cary rises from the bench to address Pendleton, reporting that the Declaration of Rights has come out of committee. Then the compact, handsome horseman reads the document to the convention.

The first article, in full, is:

> That all men are by nature equally free and independent and have certain inherent Rights, of which, when they enter into a State of Society, they cannot, by any Compact, deprive or divest their Posterity: namely, the Enjoyment of Life and Liberty, with their Means of acquiring and possessing Property, and pursuing and obtaining Happiness and Safety.

In all, there are eighteen articles. Predictably,

some evoke frowns and murmurs of dissent from the delegates and from the spectators. Civil liberties have never been won easily. Some delegates believe that several of the articles are dangerous, Article I, in particular.

In a few days, Thomas Ludwell Lee writes to his brother Richard Henry: "A certain set of aristocrats—for we have such monsters here—finding that their execrable system cannot be reared on such foundations, have to this time kept us at bay on the first line, which declares all men to be born free and independent . . . ."

The aristocrats cannot stomach the idea of the masses, the so-called "common" people, white and black, having an equal say in government. By no means is there complete agreement on the Declaration. Collision was inevitable from the moment that Mason dipped his pen into ink.

The document is read once again by Clerk Tazewell and then Pendleton orders it to be sent to the Committee of the Whole. Wednesday next is set for the opening day of full convention debate. This will allow time for copies of it to be printed, read, thought about, and discussed.

Copies are quickly forwarded to Lee, Jefferson, and Wythe in Philadelphia. The Declaration appears in the June 6th issue of the *Pennsylvania Eve-*

*ning Gazette.* The congressional delegates from the other colonies read it that night, recognizing that a profound statement on civil liberties has come from Virginia.

Now, the full attention of the Cary committee can be turned to drafting Virginia's constitution. The conservatives had proposed a constitution believed to have been written by Carter Braxton, who was unseated for his bid to the Fifth Convention but is now in Philadelphia as an alternate delegate to the Congress. The Braxton paper is put aside in favor of further work by George Mason. It is another indication that the stubborn hold of the conservatives, weakening with every month, is nearing an end.

Finally, the Declaration comes before the convention and is sent back to committee by floor objections. Robert Carter Nicholas steadfastly opposes the first sentence of Article I as being "the forerunner or pretext for civil confusion." He is speaking of the clause that declares all men free and independent.

Slavery is already beginning to be a sensitive issue. Jefferson thinks it is a terrible practice even though his constant traveling companion is the black slave Bob. Pendleton, too, maintains he hates slavery but his body servant is a black slave named Nero. Patrick Henry says, "I believe a time will come when an opportunity will be offered to abolish this lamentable evil." But he admits he keeps slaves as a "convenience." George Mason's Gunston Hall is largely run by slaves, yet he proclaims that all men are "born free and independent." A deep sense of guilt seems to run through the public statements of these men. Yet none, at this time, have freed their black slaves. It is an ugly paradox.

The Declaration is debated on the floor of the hall on June 3rd, 4th, and 5th. Now few in numbers, but still persuasive, the beleaguered opponents of certain sections of the Declaration can only "filibuster," or talk endlessly to prevent a vote.

Two days later, Richard Henry Lee submits to the Continental Congress for consideration Virginia's resolve to declare independence for all the colonies. That it will spark angry opposition and heated debate is predictable.

As Lee's voice, having already "declared the United Colonies free and independent states," trails off in Philadelphia's State House, John Adams immediately rises to second the motion, and debate begins, lasting until seven that night. Lee, Adams, and George Wythe are the chief spokesmen for passage of the resolution. Jefferson stays in the background, wisely bowing to more forceful speakers.

The primary opponents of the measure are Pennsylvanians John Dickinson and James Wilson, Robert R. Livingston of New York, and Edward Rutledge of South Carolina. Rutledge thinks that the Virginia delegates had "no power" to declare independence for all the colonies. Wilson believes that the people of the middle colonies are "not yet ripe for bidding adieu to British connection. . . ." The same words could easily have been spoken by that Tidewater blueblood, R. C. Nicholas.

The argument lasts three days in the rising heat inside the State House and then on Monday, June 10th, Rutledge proposes that a vote on the resolution be postponed until July 1st. President John Hancock then appoints a committee to draft a "Declaration of Independence" on the possibility that there might be agreement. Jefferson, John Adams, Benjamin Franklin, Roger Sherman, and Robert Livingston are named to the committee. Livingston wants no part of it and leaves for New York.

The task of writing the declaration finally goes to Jefferson. Much later, Adams is to say that he passed the job to the young, red-haired southerner for the following reasons: "Reason 1st. You are a Virginian and Virginia ought to be at the head of

this business. Reason 2nd. I am obnoxious, suspected and unpopular. Reason 3rd. You can write ten times better than I can."

Jefferson, residing at Fred Graff's house in the Quaker City, does much of the writing in the parlor, balancing a writing box on his knee. He works on the document in the evening after he returns from the day's session in the State House and in the morning before he goes off to the hall at Fifth and Chestnut streets.

He draws on Virginia's resolve for independence and Mason's Declaration of Rights as well as on his own studies in philosophy and civil liberty. The declaration is shaped and smoothed, probably with suggestions from Adams, Franklin, and Sherman.

In Williamsburg, the tiring debate on the Declaration comes to an end on the 12th day of June. Minor arguments had been made on the 10th, and now it comes to a vote on a third reading. It passes unanimously. Originally composed of eighteen articles, the bill was first cut to fourteen and now stands at sixteen. It is a remarkable document in its expressions of freedom and liberty for all people.

The men of "integrity and ability" had prevailed.

# 21 The Enchanted Ground

As the fifty days of the Fifth Convention begin to spin away, one last major job remains to be accomplished—the drafting of the Virginia constitution, the plan for government. George Mason regards it as a natural part of the Declaration of Rights, but it is in work as a separate document. It opens with an outline of the three departments that will compose the government—legislative, judicial, and executive.

Through Edmund Randolph, Jefferson has already made known his opposition to the writing of a permanent constitution at this time. He thinks the task ought to be postponed until the people have had a chance to elect representatives who can relay their views at a special constitutional convention. But Jefferson's ideas are rejected by Pendleton, Mason, and Henry. They feel that the same delegates now meeting in Williamsburg would most likely be reelected to such a convention. The drafting of the constitution proceeds.

In contrast to the Declaration of Rights, authored primarily by Colonel Mason, much of the work on the constitution is done in committee, but the committee is again steered by the man from Gunston Hall. This plan of government, to be the first such written constitution in America, and in the world, created by self-governing men, is the "rock" referred to by Edmund Pendleton.

Debate continues daily in the committee, and then on Monday, June 24th, Archibald Cary submits the constitution to the convention and floor discussion begins. With the damp heat a factor, tempers wear thin as point after point is contested. The debate lasts four days.

Patrick Henry, for instance, is absolutely opposed to the lack of veto power for the governor. He feels the governor should have the right to prevent a bill passed by the legislature from becoming law. It is another unusual position for Henry, who is beginning to show signs of conservatism. He has cheerfully done battle with British governors for years, as Lord Dunmore would certainly attest. Above all, Henry had been furious when governors overrode bills or dismissed the burgesses.

On the floor this week, he claims that the governor will become a "mere phantom" without the power of a veto. His position is voted down, though. The visage of Dunmore is still too fresh in the minds of the delegates. Governors can flaunt their authority; the delegates had been on that miserable road before.

On the 29th, Virginia's new constitution is read for the third time and passes unanimously before a near-exhausted house of delegates. The last important job done, they stream out onto Duke of Gloucester Street and retire to the taverns and coffeehouses. But even the clatter of dice and the thud of ale tankards seems weary this day.

The next day Mr. Henry is elected the first governor of the Commonwealth of Virginia, winning over Thomas Nelson, Sr. A career that had begun shakily in the Hanover Courthouse with a country lawyer's appeal to a prejudiced jury would end in the Governor's Palace. Perhaps he had had a premonition of his election when he fought to retain the power of veto for the governor.

In writing to the convention that afternoon, Henry said, in part, "I shall enter upon the duties of my office whenever you, gentlemen, shall be pleased to direct, relying upon the known wisdom and virtue of your honourable house to supply my defects, and to give permanency and success to that system of government which you have formed, and which is so wisely calculated to secure equal liberty and advance human happiness . . ."

On Sunday the bell of Bruton Church rings out to summon Williamsburg to worship. There is much to be thankful for. The people have spoken and Virginia has "abjured Allegiance to his Brittanick Majesty" as well as authored the magnificent Declaration of Rights.

Governor Henry attends the service, along with a number of convention delegates. He sits in the silk-curtained governor's pew, introducing it, at last, to non-British breeches. He has changed over the years and now he even looks like a governor. Soon he will be seen around town in a peach-colored coat, with powder in his tiewig; the former

country fiddler and storyteller will look almost elegant.

Prayers are said for the success of the deliberations in Philadelphia. Within twenty-four hours, debate on the Declaration of Independence will begin on the floor of the Continental Congress. The document has been honed and polished, worked over almost endlessly. John Adams and the members of his small committee, especially Thomas Jefferson, can well be proud of it.

But the convention in Williamsburg is all but dozing. The important work is done. The town slumps, too. The smell of honeysuckle is in the air and the wisteria has just passed its peak. Its purple blossoms are floating down. The York and James lap calmly on their shores. The tobacco and corn in the fields have the deep green color of robust health. The citizens have no knowledge, of course, of the fierce debate that is going on in the State House to the north.

George Wythe and Richard Henry Lee, home again in Williamsburg, have already reported to the convention that the chances seem good that the Declaration of Independence will be approved, though it may differ somewhat from Jefferson's original draft. John Adams will lead the way to its passage, they say.

The week falters along at old mule pace and then it is July 5th, the date set to adjourn the Fifth (and last) Virginia Convention. Pendleton takes his chair and the house is called to order for the few pieces of minor business that remain.

There is a perplexing reminder of the former power of the Crown in the morning and evening services of the Anglican Church, and the convention votes unanimously to drop the words "O Lord save the King" from the prayers. Other references to the King and royal family are struck out. Few people are of a mind to "save the King" with forty-five thousand British and German troops on the way to America.

There is something else. That man of many talents, the astounding George Mason, has designed a state seal. His description of it begins, "Virtus, the genius of commonwealth, dressed like an Amazon, resting on a spear in one hand, and holding a sword in one hand, and treading on Tyranny. . . ."

Colonel Mason's seal is adopted unanimously, and for a few minutes the delegates move about the hall, examining their new state seal or the copy of the new constitution on Clerk Tazewell's desk. Finally, a motion is made to adjourn, and the members return to their seats and quiet down. The motion carries and Edmund Pendleton stands in front of the high-backed chair on the dais to make his closing remarks.

Hugh Blair Grigsby, a historian of the day, wrote: "His handsome face, the serenity of which the fiercest storm of debate could not ruffle, reflected the unwonted feelings which agitated his bosom; and when the clear tones of that silver voice fell upon the ears of the members now for the last time, feelings too deep for utterance were excited. . . ."

Pendleton reportedly said that the delegates "had committed their cause to the God of Battles and should it be His will, as he hoped and believed it would be, to give success to their arms, what a glorious triumph awaited them."

The convention then adjourns. It is July 5, 1776, and in the small town of Williamsburg, the rebellious men begin to scatter to their homes, unaware that the Declaration of Independence has carried in Philadelphia. In fact, at this very moment, a copy is pounding toward Williamsburg by postrider.

Later, in 1778 George Mason will write, "We seem to have been standing on enchanted ground."

As usual, Colonel Mason was entirely correct.

# Prelude to Independence

Virginia's "Fifty Days" in 1776 are often called a "Prelude to Independence." Few periods in the history of any state or nation can match the momentous events that took place in Williamsburg at the Fifth Convention, from May 15th to July 5th.

Of the Declaration of Rights alone, the impact on America and free men everywhere has been lasting. The words and ideas of the sixteen articles became a part of the Declaration of Independence, and then the Bill of Rights of the United States Constitution. And the words of Williamsburg have gone far beyond the shores of America.

From the Declaration of Independence, Philadelphia, 1776: "We hold these truths to be self-evident; that all men are created equal; that they are endowed . . . with certain inalienable rights; that among these are life, liberty and the pursuit of happiness."

From the French Declaration of the Rights of Men and the Citizen, 1789: "Men are born and remain free and equal in rights . . . These rights are liberty, property, security and resistance to oppression."

From the Constitution of Uruguay, 1934: ". . . Inhabitants of the Republic have the right to be protected in the enjoyment of life, honor, liberty, security, work and property. No person shall be deprived of these rights except in conforming with the laws that may be established for reasons of general interest."

From the Venezuelan Constitution, 1947: "The Venezuelan Nation proclaims as the prime reason of its existence the spiritual, political and economic liberty of man, emphasized in human dignity, social justice and the equitable participation of all the people in the enjoyment of the national wealth."

From the United Nations Universal Declaration of Human Rights, 1948: "All human beings are born free and equal in dignity and rights. They are endowed with reason and conscience and should act toward one another in a spirit of brotherhood."

# Bibliography

BECKER, CARL, *The Declaration of Independence, A Study in the History of Political Ideas*. New York: Alfred A. Knopf, 1942.

BOYD, JULIAN P., *The Declaration of Independence*. Princeton, N.J.: Princeton University Press, 1945.

BRAND, IRVING, *James Madison, The Virginia Revolutionist, 1751–1780*. Indianapolis and New York: Bobbs-Merrill, 1941.

BRIDENBAUGH, CARL, *Seat of Empire. The Political Role of Eighteenth Century Williamsburg*. Williamsburg: Colonial Williamsburg, Inc., 1958.

CARSON, JANE, *Colonial Virginians at Play*. Williamsburg: A Colonial Williamsburg Publication, 1965.

———, *James Innes and His Brothers of the F.H.C.* Williamsburg: A Colonial Williamsburg Publication, 1965.

———, *We Were There, Descriptions of Williamsburg, 1699–1859*. Williamsburg: A Colonial Williamsburg Publication, 1965.

DOUTHAT, ROBERT MEADE, *Patrick Henry, Patriot in the Making*, Vol. I. Philadelphia and New York: J. B. Lippincott, 1957.

———, *Patrick Henry, Practical Revolutionary*, Vol. II. Philadelphia and New York: J. B. Lippincott, 1969.

ECKENRODE, H. J., *The Revolution in Virginia*. Hamden, Conn.: Archon Books, 1964.

———, *Separation of Church and State in Virginia*. New York: DeCapo Press, 1971.

FREEMAN, DOUGLAS SOUTHALL, *George Washington, A Biography*, Vol. III. New York: Charles Scribner's Sons, 1951.

FRENCH, ALLEN, *The First Year of the American Revolution*. Boston: Houghton Mifflin, 1934.

GOODWIN, RUTHERFOORD, *A Brief and True Report Concerning Williamsburg in Virginia*. Williamsburg: Colonial Williamsburg, Inc., 1941.

———, *The Record of Bruton Parish Church*. Richmond, Va.: The Dietz Press, 1941.

GREENE, JACK P., *The Quest for Power*. Chapel Hill, N.C.: University of North Carolina Press, 1963.

GRIGSBY, HUGH BLAIR, *The Virginia Convention of 1776*. Richmond: 1855. New York: DeCapo Press, 1969. (Reprint)

HILL, HELEN, *George Mason, Constitutionalist.* Gloucester, Mass.: Peter Smith, 1966.

HUME, IVOR NOËL, *1775, Another Part of the Field.* New York: Alfred A. Knopf, 1966.

LABAREE, BENJAMIN WOODS, *The Boston Tea Party.* New York: Oxford University Press, 1964.

MALONE, DUMAS, *Jefferson, The Virginian.* Boston: Little, Brown, 1947.

MAYS, DAVID JOHN, *Edmund Pendleton, 1721–1803, A Biography*, Vol. II. Cambridge, Mass.: Harvard University Press, 1952.

MILLER, ELMER I., *The Legislature of the Province of Virginia.* New York: AMS Press, 1967.

MORGAN, EDMUND S., *The American Revolution, A Review of Changing Interpretations.* Washington, D.C.: American Historical Association, 1958.

————, *Prologue to Revolution, The Sources and Documents of the Stamp Act Crisis, 1764–1766.* Chapel Hill, N.C.: University of North Carolina Press, 1959.

———— and MORGAN, HELEN B., *The Stamp Act Crisis.* Chapel Hill, N.C.: University of North Carolina Press, 1953.

*The Proceedings of the Convention of Delegates, Held at The Capitol, In The City of Williamsburg, In The Colony of Virginia, On Monday, the 6th of May, 1776.* Reprinted by a resolution of the House of Delegates, February 24, 1816. Richmond, Va.: Ritchie, Trueheart & Du-Val, Printers, 1816.

ROSSITER, CLINTON, *Seedtime of the Republic.* New York: Harcourt & Brace, 1953.

ROWLAND, KATE MASON, *The Life of George Mason, 1725–1792*. New York: Russell & Russell, 1964.

STANARD, MARY NEWTON, *The Story of Virginia's First Century*. Philadelphia: J. B. Lippincott, 1928.

TYLER, MOSES COIT, *Patrick Henry*. Boston: Houghton Mifflin, 1898.

WERTENBAKER, THOMAS JEFFERSON, *Torchbearer of the Revolution*. Gloucester, Mass.: Peter Smith, 1965.

WHIFFEN, MARCUS, *The Eighteenth-Century Houses of Williamsburg, An Architectural History*. Williamsburg: Colonial Williamsburg, Inc., 1960.

———, *The Public Buildings of Williamsburg*, Vol. I. Williamsburg: Colonial Williamsburg, Inc., 1958.

WIRT, WILLIAM, *Sketches of the Life and Character of Patrick Henry*. Philadelphia: 1817.

WRIGHT, ESMOND, *Causes and Consequences of the American Revolution*. Chicago: Quadrangle Books, 1966.

# Index

## About the Author

Theodore Taylor is the author of a number of books for young people, including *Air Raid—Pearl Harbor!*, *People Who Make Movies*, *The Children's War*, and *The Cay*, which was selected by the American Library Association as a Notable Children's Book, 1969, and also won eight other awards.

In the course of writing this history of Williamsburg prior to the American Revolution, Mr. Taylor visited the modern reconstruction of the colonial town in Virginia. "One morning," he writes, "I awakened at 2:45 A.M. to go to the Powder Magazine and spend a chilly hour at approximately the same time and on the same day in April that Lord Dunmore's raid on it took place 197 years ago. Looking around in the dead silence, through a thin mist, the James City County courthouse looming darkly across the way, I fully expected to see Lieutenant Collins and his British marines coming down Duke of Gloucester Street as they did on that morning in 1775."

Mr. Taylor lives with his wife and three children in California.

## About the Illustrator

Richard Cuffari's paintings have been exhibited in several New York galleries. A number of his illustrations have appeared in the American Institute of Graphic Arts design shows and in the Society of Illustrators annual exhibits.

A native of New York, Mr. Cuffari studied at Pratt Institute. He lives in Brooklyn with his wife and four children.